COMMUNION

❧

Primus St. John

Primus St. John

COMMUNION

POEMS 1976–1998

COPPER CANYON PRESS

Grateful acknowledgment is made to
Barbara Thomas for the use of her painting
A Fire in the Heart on the cover of this book.

The publication of this book was supported
by grants from the Lannan Foundation,
the National Endowment for the Arts, and the
Washington State Arts Commission. Additional
support was received from Elliott Bay Book
Company, Cynthia Hartwig, and the many
members who joined the Friends of
Copper Canyon Press campaign.
Copper Canyon Press is in residence with
Centrum at Fort Worden State Park.

LIBRARY OF CONGRESS
CATALOGING-IN-PUBLICATION DATA

St. John, Primus, 1939–
Communion: poems 1976–1998 /
Primus St. John.
    p. cm.
ISBN 1-55659-125-X (alk. paper)
1. West Indian American's Poetry.
2. Slave-trade Poetry.
3. Slavery Poetry. I. Title.
PS3569.A454 C66 1999
811'.54 — DC21 99-6200
            CIP

3 5 7 9 8 6 4
SECOND PRINTING

COPPER CANYON PRESS
Post Office Box 271
Port Townsend, Washington 98368
www.ccpress.org

To my family, past, present, and future –
thank you for the light.

CONTENTS

from SKINS ON THE EARTH

I   All the Way Home 5
Benign Neglect / West Point, Mississippi, 1970 7
Our Lady of Congress 8
American Roots: Moral Associations 10
Elephant Rock 12
Oluranti 15
A Splendid Thing Growing 16
He Imagined the Gorgeous Pattern of the
         New Skin and Settled for America 18
Strike One, Strike Two: A Savage Song 20
The Holy Ghost Will Not Materialize 21

II   The Violence of Pronoun 23
Water Can Only Wrap Me, but Life Must
         Hold Me 25
Eloma 26
Esom 27
For These Conditions There Is No Abortion 28
Laborer 30
Indeed 31
Bedding Down 32
The Carpenter 33
After the Truckers' Restaurant 35
Two Voices from Hester Street (1904) 36

III   Tyson's Corner 39
Constellations 40
Southern Comfort: A Gentleman 42
Lynching and Burning 44
Looking at a Bus Stop 45

Into the Open Heart   46
Survival   47
The Dark God of Roses   48

IV   The *Morning Star*   52
The Fountain   53
Field   54
Biological Light   56
Westward Expansion   58
A Poem to My Notebook, Across Winter   59
Waking   60

from LOVE IS NOT A CONSOLATION;
IT IS A LIGHT

I   *from* Postcards: A Metaphysical Journey   65

II   Love and the Healing: 2   69
Ambiguities   71

III   Lyric 4   73
Lyric 5   73
Lyric 6   73

IV   Notes on a Painter's Palette   75
Lyric 7   81
Lyric 8   81

V   Reading a Story to My Child   83
Like van Gogh, I Can't Begin in Prose   87
Turning from the *National Geographic* to Peer out
       the Window   91
Lyric 10   93
Lyric 11   95
Lyric 12   95

VI 25 Exposures 97
Lyric 13 101
Lyric 14 102

VII Ocean of the Streams of Story 104
Love Poem 4 106
Love Poem 6 106

DREAMER

I "We came to know each other" 109
"That day" 111
"When the butterflies appear" 113
"Today" 114
"I think I will make the man thin" 116
"I told her to go outside" 119
"I was to become a Bajan" 120
"What do stories do?" 121

II Dreamer 125

III That in Itself Is the Proverb 152
Sunday 154
We Are Going to Be Here Now 155
Lord, Man 157
Tale 159
Once 161
Worship 162
Focus 163
Talk 165
Dread 168
Pearle's Poem 170
Pentecostal 172
Song 173
Carnival 175

Textual Notes to Dreamer 176

IF THERE WERE NO DAYS,
WHERE WOULD WE LIVE

I After That 181
Yellow Sweet Clover 182
At Colm's Foot 182
The Waterfall 183
Anniversary 183
The Sniper 184
There Are Always Fish Here 185
Signing 186
Why 187
May, Age 2 188
Dancing with Wolves 188
Water Carrier 189
By the Mule River 190
Ripe 191
Aubade 192
Call It What You Want 193
Obsessions Are Important 194
Ironing 197
Lemon Verbena 198
Ars Poetica 199
¿Qué Pasa? 200
All This 201
The End of the Beginning of the Story 202
Nelson 203
Maps 204
Kindling 204
Good Night 205
Things That Are Like Butterflies 205
Fire Starters 206
Lists 206
Teo & Monacita 207

Getting Ready to Talk about Metaphors & Similes
    on Valentine's Day   208
A Story   209
Listening to the Curandera   210
Wind   211
The Marathon   211
The Wily Cover-Thief's Tale   212

11   If There Were No Days, Where Would
        We Live   214

About the Author   233

COMMUNION

Primus St. John

from

SKINS ON THE EARTH

I

*"Though we do not believe it yet,
the interior life is a real life, and
the intangible dreams of people have
a tangible effect on the world."*

All the Way Home

The lamps hung like a lynching
In my town.
It was a dark town.
In a dark town,
Light is a ragged scar.
Fright begs that ragged scar.
It begs doorways.

I love that town.
From its lean men
I learned
Emotion;
And how to hold that fine edge,
That makes us
        people...

Mrs. Blackwell's
Sold her house.
Since her husband revolved his head,
She wears bright hats
That speak to people.

B.J.'s doing time.
His children betray that time,
By the breathing it takes
To dream through windows.
Mary Lee dreams him letters;
She dreams by heart...

Now I feel a new scar.
I've left home
And leaned so far,
I'm almost zero.

And though it's lonely,
Whatever knowing is,
It strings a long fine wire.
At night I lie awake
And listen to that wire –

All the way home.

Benign Neglect/West Point, Mississippi, 1970

Suppose you were dreaming about your family,
And when you woke up
You found a man named Sonny Stanley
Had just shot you (5 times),
Or justice
Looked just like the color your blood was running –
Running wild in the world –
But the world wouldn't see.
Then
You read, somewhere
(I think it's the papers),
If it's a problem, Boy,
We don't have one here;
We don't ask a man to die
Like groceries babbling froth to flies.
But bleeding,
You watch your neighbors
Write away to their windows to
Hide! Hide!
   "He's not there. He's not there."
The last sentence?
The last sentence is your *Father* –
One of the windows...
   "He's not there. He's not there."

   Good-bye, Johnny.

Our Lady of Congress

The opposition likes dry poems –
No storms
That are holding hands
The same way
It begins to rain
When we suspect our lives.
The answer to everything
Is a just peace
(So we elected him president),
Or better umbrellas
That are not afraid.
It is an aesthetic form
History has taken,
To adjust time to a seashell
When strong water comes.
So we go back on our lives.
Reliving all of our curves when we were worms.
Caution, inside
Never learns
No poem is listening to our
Lives –
This way,
Not even the earth.

Justice is in stones
With thirst.
Large storms live on weight
And look our way
When the seals are broken.
Water is success
Whispered to stone like slime.
What we are behind our faces
Is a crack that's leaking,

A yell that's lost its body in a shell.
There are no more words
For old Yankee faces like ours
But the luck we have left.

American Roots: Moral Associations

1   Kinship:
    Is embarrassing the wind,
    Like dead black boys,
    Falling down from the trees,
    Then downstream –
    On their knees,
    Blood like,
    Like a rich nation.

2   Metaphor:
    Becomes humiliating,
    And clean,
    Ticking like a ripe machine.
    Do not
    Bend,
    Fold,
    Or mutilate me –
    This is your future speaking.

3   The air smells so metaphysical
    We have accused it –
    Of smog,
    And lost manhood,
    Then all ritual.

4   Whoever wrote:
    A view is a mountain speaking
    But left the introduction
    For the snow,
    And accused silence
    Of its soul.

5   The whole nation:
Is a stanza of blackness,
A huge white whale,
Faith in space
(Like the newspapers),
And the quiet insistence
We have peace,
And it's your world, brother.

We take place in what we believe.
I've memorized that
                    Because
It's life
        And that
Invisible –
If you're thinking in the dark.

Take the line we drew
Around   Elephant Rock,
            A beginning
That could happen
            Any day
You put your thumb
                Down
That long block
And saw all neighbors
            As trees.

On our side
We kept these
        Possibilities:
            1. Mount up now
            2. You're ten
            3. This country is your trail too

We began to see
Near this rock
            What did not look right
In our books,
            That presence
Was enough
And

Anyone who worked
Should be free
        To meet himself—
Sometime.

We called it
Cowboys and Indians
               Or
The girls should stay home
It's safe that way.
But every day this
        Mythology
Grew
We'd lose time
And we'd lose.

One day, Jerry said
Believe—
      Go ahead
         Believe.

We tried—
To keep the thin trails,
Old trees,
But there's something wrong
        With America—
If you're Black
Believe—
      Go ahead
         Believe.

These three were the most creative:
      Breno Jones
      He left five kids,
      And a thin, incredible wife.

Duke
He was never lucky,
He just died
&
Jerry too,
OD'd
At the feet of Elephant Rock...

And because even this is not enough,
Something else
Over their heads
That still takes place
In America.
Old walls
&
Tall rocks
With that sign
I could never understand –
JESUS SAVES

Oluranti

Planting roses,
History comes back.
Moses was a strange man.
He pitched tents,
And saved rocks
Like God told him to grow old.
Now that the mud is shared,
By both my knees
I look out for that country.
A river comes from the north.
What happened out there
Took forty years;
Most of us slept,
Couldn't hear,
Blamed the rain
For the threatening edges.
Night after night
Most of us walked,
Talked in our sleep...
There were no roses,
But he waited.

A Splendid Thing Growing

Chair:
It is the name of me.
The ending of my arms
And the ending of my legs
Mean nothing.
I cannot creak enough.

Dish:
It is the emptiness.
I am going to breathe
Over the edge,
And feel –
Louder.

Vase:
And water are righteousness.
So flowers are given,
So dance,
And wind
       within us.

Cup:
It is the round place.
So is intention.
So is our drinking.

Godliness:
That is knife.
Given decision.
Given harshness
       like cut.

Table:
Be with me
On this earth.
It is set with our flesh.

Come closer:
Like carpet
And trust.
Dust in us
Everything woven.

Drapes:
They are disturbances,
And thinking.
Flapping making no sense,
But storms.

Doom:
It is always left.
At night,
It is a splendid thing growing.
It shows us nothing.

O Nouns! Forgive us.

He Imagined the Gorgeous Pattern of the New Skin and Settled for America

The quiet which is my wife endures:
I have hurt nothing, unless we have touched.

It is the indicative mood,   after desire
The Deerslayer

Now middle-aged
Has become lonesome and white again

Rising up out of the continent
That is Chingachgook

Red-skinned, red-eyed morning light
The myth that has happened to the democratic.

That Black man over there:
Slaughtered in the hills of my wife...

Imagination
Black and breathing.

I   am slaughtered in his wife
It has happened to meaning.

Fit to be Satan – now:
Cooper, Hawthorne, Melville's

I wear my dark-skinned hat –
Irreconcilable

In the final phase. Satanic
It seems to fit me right.

To walk away alone
Into the sunset of our bleeding children.

Strike One, Strike Two: A Savage Song

I am as safe as I can
Slide into the softball game (Sunday).
Nothing happens to men
But the phallic deed.
The tight hands around the bat
Like a negative
(Mother, print that).

Beer is savage, at last, I am delivered.
In a year's fat, or two,
I will be pregnant enough
To go home.

Over the years,
I have elected the men
Unpassionate enough
To understand that.
Lately, out of sheer myth
They're fucking up.

You've got to pitch the ball in
Like a gun rack
Floating across an imperfect pickup.
Brush the coloreds back from my wife
(I mean life).
Darling, I look forward to seeing you (Sunday).
The metaphor is *put it here babe*
                 put it here babe
                 put it here.

The Holy Ghost Will Not Materialize

This poem:
Fire of thighs, the breathing wind,
And me big pioneer
Is uncouth.
I want to sleep at night, mix the metaphors,
Stark dumb
My impression of the unconscious.

The loveliest woman
Is cruel iron.
I beat the forge of her soul
Pregnant, with war.

The trouble with Time
Is it's organic.
It means she bleeds.
Blood ruins everything.
Blood

Blood,
I'm going to war
Backwoodsman alone in paradise
in the name of the father,
the son, and the ghost.

"*This is the meal equally set,*
this is the meat for
natural hunger."

The Violence of Pronoun

1   Loving came her way,
          Vicious.
  It rose up,
  From the earth,
  And made her father's hand,
  Around her throat,
  A bird of prey,
  And carried her away—
          In mind,
  Like a limp patient.
  He was not drunk.
  It is worse.
  In this world,
  We cannot feel...

2   In my sociology class—
          For understanding
  Black folks—
  They tried to understand
  Our lives—
          Like buckshot.
  What we have done,
          To love
  Is unforgivable.
  They took our rakes
  And treated us like dirt.
  It was so perfect,
  They asked for grades.

3   Leaving people out of this—
  I can forgive.
  I married her anyway,

And in the church,
When I unfolded her hand,
          I saw

In her palm
The way she would die...
Leaping out of democracy,
Through some weird window,
          White
With the wilderness of God –
          1965, Memorial Day.
And I went on, crazy
          At first,
And crazy even now
For being so unmilitant...

4   What I told that class,
     (You know) they said it hurt.
     "It is our innocence
     That makes us vicious."

Water Can Only Wrap Me,
but Life Must Hold Me

A Black man, from Oklahoma,
Married moisture.
Her name was Ruth.

Whenever he talked a stone
Cracked for water,
But not for doom.

Over the years she has become
Sweeter, listening
Like a horned toad:
At nights,
Wearing only her own
Horned toad clothes —
But breathing
As strong as they fit her.

It has been years…
Love and exposure have become a poem.

Eloma

We have not built the train
Here, our tracks are our own steel
Storms.

At night, we build the right fire
And watch the smoke –
That emphasizes things.

He ordered me like a book
He has read aloud:
Unresolved, without refuge.

I came to him for miles
On the hips of wagon
To be *unowned.*

Ever since the days of cotton
I have been unredeemed.
Whitmanesque as the bells
I go to my wanderer

Possessed.

Esom

Many things in one are black.
I want to emphasize the soil –
Black
Irony against unnamed pain.

I have dreamed of a wilderness
Called Woman,
Her black knees with ash
Part soil, part rain
Where I can find the root of things

Like Name:
Full and rounded and unredeemed.

We will call our way *seed*
Like children again

Our impact on the smoke.

For These Conditions There Is No Abortion

1 They say the tongue is only *Praxis*.
   It is only a surge forward
   Between Spring and God.
   Months later,
   God is gone. Our spring is upon us.
   We learn the names for children;
   They don't want us or our child.
   We are just sophomores and curses.
   Like Aristotle
   I believe plot after plot
   Means something.
   It is a formula evening:
   The sun is red
   Night is someone beyond blue
   Her belly is living and dying
   And we don't sit close anymore —
   Even in the lunchroom.
   Her eyes are smooth stones, falling.
   I am a man
   Therefore I am falling.
   She says today she has learned a word
   For folks like us;
   I am about to say sorry
   She says *pathos*...

2 Martha's story is not so simple (*yes*).
   She is older and freer
   Like her lover is gone (*yes*)
   And she is poor (*yes*),
   Poor Martha:
   With her belly in her hands
   With a man who is anything but Jesus.
   Poor Martha:

With blood and misunderstanding
Tragedy is opening for all her roses.

Lord, legalize this:
Our bloom and decay.

Martha is something in common with rope
On fire.
Her womb should give her pleasure,
Not *hangers* and *quinine* and *soda.*

Laborer

I work for what I get.
I get words.
I take them out the rent—
In hate.

I come home late,
It does not work.
She listens to me
Like germs.

I am so drunk
My shoes are cracked.
She will go away
Through the openings,
Taking nothing.

Of all the colors,
I know,
Black is the most truthful
To her children.

Indeed

I married a girl in the summer who slept on the beach.
I married her feet, sandlike, and gathered her limbs.
These dreams,
Flesh, are so remote, about 500,000 years in darkness.
A loss crows would seek repose in in the shudders of the
                                                    earth
And become dancers.
Each day I am amazed at stones. They hear me. They
                                                    break
Into our children, are ruined again and again to grow,
                                                    but
Baked bread crumbs – resounding their lives like brooms.
Indeed I think I have made a move – from thighs,
To silence, to you. It is a good one.

Bedding Down

The redness of the apples
Cannot see,
I understand
In the night-black air
The smells of no fear —
Breathing,
Just the crackling
Of bent limbs in hidden places.
I smell the reasons,
They are all sweet,
Pitch-black,
Unknown.
I go down on my hands,
And on my knees,
And shed my skin —
For health,
And spend the night.

The Carpenter

1   I look at my hands
    In a dark hour.
    They are my wife,
    Another life,
    Fawnal,
    Explicitly made.
    I compare responsibility
    To journey:
    They are pitch-black
    Whirling in the outside world
    Left behind like a native –
    Possessed.

2   We are older:
    Toil is our long way
    Back home.
    It works.
    Causes the space to beat
    Like a heart.
    It is a part of the poem
    That appears
    And appears on its own.
    It goes on
    On its own,
    Mystical as evil
    But, it is called freedom.

3   I'm sorry:
    I was telling you about my hands.
    How well we are married.
    It follows,
    I recognize all truth
    As some part of ten.

Spirit is my thumb,
Passionately.
Without thumb
I would be nothing.
I have met some who believe in reason.
They have had too much wine,
Confess cause and effect—
It has been painful.

4 I told you it is unreasonable:
I guess I should say here,
I am your carpenter.
Ethnically, dark wood
Is my life.
I could show you my story better,
Sanding,
Then when I speak
You would hear
                    Africa
                    Africa
One more thing, my love.
I have discovered in this dark wood
A skill you have called our loneliness.
I sand it down for you
Until our bodies fall off.

After the Truckers' Restaurant

Men look at curves in the dark,
With both their eyes.
Any line that is a turned mouth –
In the sides of a mountain,
        Truckers believe,
You can turn to a nerve
In that mouth
That screams so no one hears it.

In sleeping,
My woman breathes a sign
On the window,
About zeros blinking
        (She's trusting).
To touch that trust
I trace my hand
Where all zeros come from.

I am a man as black
As the black of every curve
That awaits me.
My headlights are on
        (High beam, if that can help),
And I hear voices
Coming from all of the spots
I will never see
        Off the roads in the dark.

Whatever I will do tonight,
That's coming too.
I can hear it.
She can hear it (sleeping).

Two Voices from Hester Street (1904)

1   This morning
In the warm air,
I paint the sheets out
My window
That beat my life
Until I am mad
In the dry hand
Of clothespins.

I am a psalm
In this new land –
Like a barn filled with wheat
And flies.
My white-skinned music
Grins, lost, in the air.

2   *I see her hair*
I see her hair –
Sing.
The blackbirds are wild.
They declare
They declare
The common things.
The famine and the grin,
In the eyes of the poor.
Their wings are unreachable
Strands,
They tear my life –
Raw
Wife this morning,
Controlled like the vegetables
Downstairs
Down in the bins

Down in the bins
Speechless
And religious with the crowds
Is my love for her.

If I could take the crows
Of her hair
With me
Down the stairway
And hang them in front of me
For the darkness,
Something we have suspected
Would rise up in our hands
Would say
        Abraham
        Abraham

III

"And there was this adult pain
Down deep in the soul
Because of which was laughter."

Tyson's Corner

We were as tough as our glasses.
Wires
That bend around packages
As tight as questions;
Sometimes,
Too tight like mistakes we've made.

When the cop said:
All that blood, son, is your father,
To a boy just like us;
We looked over our rims for some mistake –
Any mistake,
But the barber didn't make one.
He'd cut that time
As deep as true feelings.

Ronnie and I were thin then...
And sure.
Dracula, would never come for us...
Not us.
But we made a promise:
        For this blood
        For the whole world's
We made a promise.

Constellations

Nighttime.
'Fore I go to bed,
Grandma say,
Put the water to your head...
Shoo
Grandma ole
She say what she want to
And folks say it all true.
What is true...
Face all wet
'Fore I sleep.
But,
Later on
In my bed
By the window,
I tug the quilt
Tight as the lights out...
Shoo
I look 'cross all the roofs I know
Feeling brave,
But the roofs ain't brave.
Farther out I see the bear—
Bear don't scare me—
Dip down
Deep in the blue water
O' Grandma's God.
I hear Grandma snore, loud,
But the bear he won't move.
He stopped there
With the water on his face.
His child nearby,
By a million years too...
Shoo

What going on that they do
What Grandma say.
Everybody know
Grandma ole.

Southern Comfort: A Gentleman

1   Evenings
The sky turns blood,
And air
Begins to bleed
Down the broken sticks
Of the bent roads.
The world is soft,
Coming off,
Don't say a word.
It's complicated—
The ways of the roofs of the shacks
Are all dull money,
And hope—
To collect.
There are children,
There is history,
There are words,
There is life
And there is the hungry moon.

2   I own this farm:
So well,
The tin lights are swinging
In my soul.
If this metaphor is not lonely,
Sell all my black feet
And their children's children,
Sell history,
Then the religion that grows white
In the fields,
Sell that
Goddamned self-sufficiency—

Until it's quiet here
And I'm free.

3   Customs come back
To the window.
I'm drunk,
Or soft
Like the chains on the roots
Of cotton.
For life I smoke
And make ghost.
Singing on Sunday,
Those Black songs
Are flying again,
Their wings beat like more men
Are coming,
Or lost.

Lynching and Burning

Men lean toward the wood.
Hoods   crease
Until they find people
Where there used to be hoods.
Instead of a story,
The whole thing becomes a scream
    then time, place, far,
    late in the country,
    alone,
    an old man's farm.
Children we used to call charcoal,
Now they smell that way—deliberately,
And the moon stares at smoke like iced tea.

Daughter,
    Once there was a place we called the earth.
    People lived there. Now we live there...

Looking at a Bus Stop

Water is just a five-letter word.
Because it is wet,
Late: thoughts let us men
Wait, impatiently,
As orange as the bus is
Not on time.
Down the street,
The trees are making mistakes
About something.
Their words are only the leaves
That are left, skeptical
As bones
And the same color
That autumn hurts.

Into the Open Heart

The way the willow trees
Hang in the fog:
Arms down,
Arms down so far
I know there are personal reasons
That can turn and become –
Old dogs' tails,
But I can't figure suffering out...
Finally, who can
Think that far
Into the open heart?
What is there about love and infirmity
That makes things happen.

Survival

Where is my father?
Black got the man,
Deep inside,
All by himself.

The Dark God of Roses

It rains like this
      Every day
And we only call it pain.
It is so invisible
It knows our names
            To the bone,
And wet
We've let the dirty street
Beat out this story.

Warren
If I see your father, first
I'll kill 'im.
That's what gone means.
      So what
Grandma told me,
Don't act like God,
He's not that blind.

Blind
That's poverty, bad teeth
And peanut-butter sandwiches,
They look like your *momma*
Your burnt-out *momma*.

Dark
Like a church inside,
Bourboned
In stained glass
On this earth
On her knees
Like all of us, here…

A garden of blood
In new Canaan.
Don't be afraid of it all.
You came and you go
Like a rose.
O Grandma
She's only a rose.

I know this rose
Made up her mind, now,
And paid for it,
And paid
So much.
Her bones were as silly
As old railroad track.

O Grandma!
The images in this rose.
American
And kitchened,
The way Miss Anne said
She never loved it,
Lately,
And it is still a mistake
Deeper than her face.

Well,
It's too late.
Warren!
Your *momma* should be president
And unpaid
And I'll be damned if she can't
Survive
Baby after baby
With the vengeance of welfare.

Not innocent
Not rich
Not free
Not even with her consciousness raised.

IV

"Turn to the center given
and do the best you can."

The Morning Star

Rumors open up
Way down the road.
The leaves include everything
Like they're really smart.
Then there is an old car
That runs on real red smoke
When the porch goes *thump*.

Mr. Anderson delivers the *Star*s
And never has to say anything.

I vote for Mr. Anderson.

The Fountain

There is always some fountain
Where the water that's really pouring –
Is our lives.
When I hear it,
I believe in all of the storms –
Where it came from.
Then I make believe
I am one of those mossbacked prophets
Who stick on stone and wait
For everything – quietly.

"We are all pouring toward the same conviction,"
I hear the fountain say,
"But we believe that, separately,"
So I believe it all –
The whole thing's that mindless,
And today is spring.

Field

1   The day needs curtains
So the wind uses butterflies,
But there is no one at home
Like the buttercups,
Who come by their yellow decisions
Again and again
To see you.
Evenly around, the temporary edges
Of apples, like children,
My face becomes accustomed to sudden
Endings of rain;
And I slosh again,
Descending, gracefully,
Looking for worms.

2   At social gatherings,
Worms eat apples and read my books.
If they had feet,
I could call them Charlemagne.
Sunlight conquers the grass
By flashing blades,
Once in a while
I crack a twig –
To prove the shade is suffering.

Charlemagne, who needs you!

3   A river is a mouth.
When it screams,
Fish disappear.
I touch my reel, uncomfortably,
And call the tension, Brother.
Huddlers in the deep

Meet the same broken dreams
On land we call unreasonable.
I go back to read,
And repeat,

Charlemagne, who needs you!

4   Lock the gate, like you're the owner
Behind the pasture;
Take your time reaching the car,
Use your life,
Understand the fish you've caught,
The worms they ate who read,
And poor Charlemagne.

Biological Light

We live here to eat;
Things stare at us.
Those things eat.
We call all of this hunger
The world.
Why?
Because we live here...

All over the world
Morning light is still happening
Like God.
It is so hard to tell
Who eats the plants first—
        Insect or crepuscular.

The wind feels the smallest birds
It's got.
If that is what we are,
It's not a lot—
Here comes the fox.

Noon: circles logically like the hawk.
God moves the rim around
Until the fox is in.
Now the fox is the hawk
And all the small things he ate
Believe him...

I have come here late;
The deer look like they have gone,
But thorns remind me
More is going on.

Gradually, memory sets the table back,
I have come from,
Across the water, as far back
As I can know.
Friends there have eaten me;
Now I stand here, that torn by hate
As I myself have eaten them.

Late; the owls say *whooo*
For what more will surely come.
Finally, I am older—
But not enough—
Surrounded by what I know
Is falling back toward the grass
More like luck than hope...

I am just lying here
Thinking this is my sleep—
How cold it is outside.
If we were fish where it is very dark
It would also be so easy:
Light would come from the dead things that we eat.

Westward Expansion

When they built these towns
Between the logs
The Indians stared.
Everyone knows, why, now.

The uprisings have come and gone.
Everyone looks backward –
Through the snow,
The answer is cold,
They were merciless,
Everyone knows, why, now.

If some hand, a claw, still scratching,
Remains,
It is in an empty hole.
A medicine man said it – long ago:
The God of this is awful.
Everyone knows, why, now.

       The truth
In country like this
Where you drive the roads
Through winter, slowly
In chains,
Is the savage painted just like passion
Was only loneliness...

Listen...

Hear how toothless it was
When Natty Bumppo died.

A Poem to My Notebook, Across Winter

The flock of birds takes shape.
           If there is faith
In the world, today
It is scattered, and the space
Is lonely,
High up there, and cold.
           The leader
– I am afraid of these birds –
Thumps for things...
This is hope   or
It is not a poem.
The tradition keeps flapping,
           Wrong,
Across the sun,
Obtrusively like an author's intervention.
It's incomplete, rich experience,
But the best tip yet is dipping,
Then diving, deep to the left...
           I hope

Waking

1   Neither is the case:
Good or *Morning.*

Actually it is the color of the air,
Red as the law.
The crime-green trees
Not moving,
Condemned by the birds.

2   If I were judge
I'd do this — *seek patience.*

What happens to the things we love...
They are here
They are not here
Like insects, they shame us
With their wings.

The clear meaning of them.
The nascent wisp.

3   I go right out the door:

If I am allowed free play, reader,
The light on my skin will be moved
Like a young horse.
I will not notice the froth
In her mouth from patience —

I will not notice.

4　　At the end of the lawn
　　　One day,
　　　In one of those stories
　　　One day,
　　　About these bright flowers
　　　The wood chips, soaked
　　　　　　　　　　　Acid
　　　And absolute –
　　　Who knows how much time we could have
　　　But just in case

　　　I Love You.

from

LOVE IS NOT
A CONSOLATION;
IT IS A LIGHT

I

"Gullibility is the key
to adventure."

from *Postcards: A Metaphysical Journey*

Dear Folks,

(Smile)
Enclosed, is the Ordinary River.
It is called "That Devil,"
In whose name the locals are baptized.
Finally that river twists
Like a hurt thing –
They say it's nothing.
It has become a new road
In a naked place.
Then, I am nothing
And it is that dream
I dreamed I dreamed.

Sincerely,

Hello,

I have just passed "Doubt,"
It is near "Milk Teeth,"
And "Nothing," and "Falling Out."
There are flowers and evidence
Of ambiguous winds.
"Doubt" is like a man
Walking in his sleep, seriously.
Offhand, it reminds me
Of a Jamesian novel
With the motives, the motives, the motives.

Have Mercy,

Say,

To get to Innocence,
You take the narrow trail
From Deep.
You squeeze into the mountain's waves.
If you meet savage rock,
It is the wrong way.
Turn left...
There, then, in our hearts'
Honeymoon, lay I.

Queequeg

J.P.,

Today is Friday.
We are still on the hill
Called Spirit of the Wind
But we are down real low
Like new flame
Just to be close.

Dad

Baby G.,

Sunday,
And what you are probably babbling
I seem to see,
(I.e.) at 60 mph
This is the alfalfa field
Of my heart.
There is no museum here,

And in a convertible,
Where birds can sing,
Anything is possible.

Dad

❧

Milton,

There is a mountain called Can
She is blind with snow
But all seers are blind
What we need
In the morning when we always see her
And are always reborn
Is a magnificent horn
And the strangely uneven voice
Of her life

Thanks,

❧

Bill,

I checked this out...
You know that ridge up there
Is north, because you know
For no reason (except this).
A great wind blows.
Behind it, the stars come out
Virtually human.
And here you are, apparently
Crude, like the sound
Of a breaking string
That seems to come from the sky.

So Long,

II

"There is no abstract art;
you must start with something."

Love and the Healing: 2

Into the world of light and air,
O Lord.
Into the world of lakes
And streams,
Mountains –
Browsing like a cow,
Singing like a child.
Hand me my duty.
Hand me my grief;
I have desire.

This is the time of power.
The rite of my blood,
The early light suffered,
The torture –
Powerful as the stars.
This is the time
Looked down a river
I've taken part in,
The hard current of feelings,
The unrequited and the magnificent,
Love.

Cold and somewhat tired.
The narrow gorge,
The reluctant simplicity
Present at death.
I think of her cheeks –
The flowering earth.

An idea:
One of these brief snatches
Is grief.

Asleep.
I hold in my hand
An infinite stone.
What am I to say?
Like her
It is smooth.

I pour the water.
The night frost
Has white hair;
I see her kissed

I see fire.
Astonished,
I don't move
I remember her lips.

Sit down;
I love you.
I say this,
I have faltered in the wind.

Please give me ointment
Thin as your body.
Don't say anything.
We have lived.

I knew I was going to die.
I pursued my life —
The aim of love.
It is tempting to cry out once,
And then awake,
But every creature has a hiding skill
A warrior can use.

Ambiguities

I call it dress
Flaring at the open window
Like an unspeakable story.
I call it lovely
Thinner than you are
Softer than your breast.
It is not peculiar.
It is not a size of fruit
But a sweetness.

Drowning in the street beside you
Drowning in our Black ghosts
Our long, dark names
I want to go dancing
I want to go dancing.

III

Lyric 4

You have finally danced.
And so it goes, *applause,*
Because the leaves need you.

Lyric 5

You think you are going somewhere
Because desire is a new direction.

Lyric 6

In the judgment of the Qur'an,
We are awake
And they call this wandering.

IV

*"For the sixteenth-century
mystic, darkness was a spiritual
opportunity — not merely the
absence of light. In the shadows of
Baroque paintings, the substance
of the soul made itself felt."*

Notes on a Painter's Palette

1   The opening paragraph of the spirit
takes risk.

We use a palette for this,
but it is transparent.

Well, you know
some people like to lay it down

and clean it out –
like fish.

No stigma is attached.

Even today, we find nothing
accomplished

that has not lain
in the possible range of graphic art –

Smeared on, shaded
in with the chalk
and spattered.

I see how deeply we must have failed,
unless it happens
we were not human.

2   I am doing this for you.
     The light says *marriage.*

     Always   Always

     And my life here
     does not end
     in the luminosity of a brush
     drawn in from the blackness
     the mysterious movements
     of which we have always guessed.

3   I live it out
     like a leaf.

     I come now to the numb thing
     that ought to be God

     we observe
     from behind the gay
     and pure play of the absolute.

4   Someone will cry out
     the loss of an ear

     A certain stiffness before the journey
     will find its voice

     Lord,
     no bird can sing this way

     I look at the white canvas
     primed like an expurgated thought

Is my father there
like a man in his sleep
like marriage
like a boy whistling for his dog?

I have never seen anything like it
before

It is, perhaps, Absalom
Or the thematic curse of Ham
Or the dignity and immense madness of children

And for the sake of atmosphere and tone,
like van Gogh
I rage for everything.

5   There is no stroke
like the ambiguous air.

The bear rolls over
and goes to sleep.

Like a grown man,
I stay awake and listen.

Ignorance is as powerful as the moon.
It makes the tides move.
It wounds the shore.

I hear the dark things done
against trees
rattle like the names
of lost slaves —

For example:
I hear my daughter grow…

"Thou must conquer thyself;
is that a difficult thing to do?"

I am a painter, Primus,
in the years following Mercy

instead of the dark
and limited wilderness outside.

6   In the woods,
I laid you.

We discussed what we are
by the fractured imagination of the moon.

In the surrounding darkness,
it all came true.

Despite hunger,
we found the bitter taste.
Lovers are mystics.

Tonight, however,
the stars are like babies
born out of wedlock,
and I want to be with you
just as they are.

7　This
Is the season
I
Call
Rain
And all I say
Is here you are
And the drops
Open their mouths
And take these oaths
I do　I do
And if in the end
Like an interjection
On the ground
I
Feel
Married
Then marriage is strange
For I am not alone
Heaping up meaning
Ambivalent
Emotive
Sharing response
Scholarly (sometimes)
But difficult
Passionate
And always
Always
Slightly afraid
For this is the season
When I am only reached
In terms
Of what I am
And I hold out my hand
And I paint

And I paint
And I paint

8   Who are you
to be so close
glistening
to mean something
outlined
as I do
take my palette
knowing as hungry wolves know
I must have something.

Lyric 7

This story is about land;
The woman with the perfect face.

Lyric 8

You have loved me
Like a bat flying in the darkness.
You have awakened me
Like a loaf of bread.

V

"The last word is never said about complex thoughts and feelings, but when we write we hope to make at least a little progress in the difficult but rewarding job of talking about our responses."

Reading a Story to My Child

This is a small boy
In a ragged coat.
Moving through his world
Is a bold paintbrush
Briefing on the light in the dark.

In the most subtle way
You are drawn to the heart
Because the heart is the name
Of the story,
But you do not know this yet.

He is going to school:
Though you know he must first
Cross the lake,
Whistle to the birds,
And clean out an understanding path
In the tall grass.

He is a good boy
Who adores crows;
He even talks like them.

He is no fool;
He will not hurt you.
He does not talk;
He lives an honest life.

At school, the children
Abhor him.
They see clothes
And the disaster of no voice.

What kind of school is this
That abhors true love?

He may not eat much,
But they are starved.
Boy, you are in the tall grass
And the soil is ruthless.

What do they teach here
That is as nice as our eyes closed?
The school is on a strange page
Farther away than the lines of the smallest trees.
And each parted brushstroke
Is like a squadron of geese.

But the little boy
Holds onto his heart.
(*Yes Sir*) It is better than a bright nickel,
Or a ball,
Or a tall pole.

He does not know
Quite how to write.
He thinks language
Is a series of bizarre pictures.

Though it is loud
It is not sharp like a crow's voice CAW CAW CAW.
And it is not bright
Like a birthday of new flowers.
(*Yes Sir*)
In all of the fields that he knows,
These pictures are not wise –
And he knows this.

At a certain point, there is more
Color on the page
Than in the eyes of a dove
That is listening.

He looks out of the window –
Home.
Someone there who knows him –
Softly and hard
Sees our storm;
Its ruthlessness
And its subtle tentacles of rain
We have all absorbed.

Hey,
But this is a boy who holds on.
My, you'd want to know this boy.
Now I am on page 8
And afraid for my soul.
At this point I say,
Boy.
(*Yes Sir*)
I say, Boy
Hold on for us all.

But today, he is given a brush.
He has climbed all the way down
And he has climbed back up
On his strange way that gets here,
And because he is not afraid
Darkness does not hide him.
He knows its crows
And their love is prehistoric

Like shale at the gorge,
Like evening cold,
Like the lonely gills of a fat fish
At the edge of water.

My, my, my,
You'd love this boy
Just for how it feels.

He paints birds at that
Exact moment flight enflames us.
He sees their heads as small prayers
On the lips of the sky.

(*Yes Sir*)
He knows how – this boy;
He knows how their wings are
Soft, ironic smiles that are alive.

My, my, my,
How Daddy cries. (*Yes Sir*)
This here is just a boy he knows
And won't say why.
A small boy
In a ragged coat.

Like van Gogh, I Can't Begin in Prose

1 Dear Milton,

Rain. But when you are here, alone, what does it
mean. It means psalm–that song sung to the harp.
Like trees, we too hold on to the earth–pull and
twang for another tongue. *It* (whatever *it* is, and
who knows that) is a sacred song. *It* is strange for
we are the ones who glorify mystery with our arms.
We call it testament because it pries at our souls
with many branches, and so you say with a huge
eye, we must practice our art like the third stomach
of a cud-chewing animal:

> *"Myrtle, Woodbine, Appletrees, Trillium,*
> *here they are, the strength of your arm*
> *stalls at the open gate of the stars.*
>
> *Feel everything, trust everything!"*

We are always limited to what we ask for (so why
not ask for wings). Therefore, desire becomes a flight
marker. For surely we hover over what we have done
as though we have wings–looking for signs that will
tell us where to go, and if we have gone somewhere,
what it means. Milton, like David of old, like David
of old or any child, we live on the tip of that lean
tongue of invocation with our sling, saying:

> *"I am small in this bright cataract of pine.*
> *I stand on the smallest stone.*
> *I am a standing prairie dog*
> *praying for my song."*

And so we have come to know: what is sacred is the storm, how the winds shimmer in the pool… how "the brushes are frightened."

Milton, it is right to say:

> *"I'm lucky, I'm always lucky."*

for though

> *"Now, somewhere, as if I were really holy,*
> *I know that my savior is lonely."*

you also know

> *"The wind has given me its child to hold—*
> *riding on my shoulders with its stars."*

Of course I'm biased; what's a friend for! But I think you have done what you should have done—gone to the fountainhead and glorified in psalm.

It may please you to know that out there, rain, too, gives in large quantities.

Love to family,

2   Dear Love to Family,

> *"O mother, momma,*
> *how can I eat this?*
> *My teeth are in my grave,*
> *my promises broken."*

On that anvil called home, we beat out family. It is enough and lovely to learn from our own. To say, *"Grandma Celia"*… to say, *"Davey, Davey… Paula, my Paula."*

On that anvil called home, we are like van Gogh
–thinking always in vivid colors that are both silent
and raging. For without it we would have no capac-
ity for peace – or war. We would be unable to settle
or plan, or to love and fear tales.

This is the center that allows us to pass among
people – the beautiful black night with all the stars...

3   Dear Beautiful Black Night with All the Stars,

Swimming in the pool it occurs to you, *"I am no one
else."* In this context, completely surrounded, every-
thing must live.

4   Dear Everything Must Live,

No country, no culture, no person, can give us more
than the "rant of the ordinary life."

5   Dear Rant of the Ordinary Life,

What we hand to our children is our truth. As large
as we are, it is small. Fragile in a bed, you learn
about infirmity's strong arms:

> *"What is it? Who's there?"*

Your heart is the real house you breathe in. Old
love's fantasy is there; it has young feet:

> *"It is strange:
> I want to weep."*

We are never at peace. Because, all our work comes
back. It spies on us as round as the moon:

"Boy, look at the moon!
Look at that moon!
It looks like it's right
On top of us."

6   Dear Right on Top of Us,

Around us, life and death. Someone born like us –
gone. Blackburn, like a magician's stroke of the
wand – gone.

   On a freighter, you stare into the water and go to
your ancestral home. You think about small Selma,
all the occupied zones we are, how our fingertips are
almost like birds.

   Once, when you were a boy, you let go of the
fence. You are still falling.

7   Dear You Are Still Falling,

You are a cantor whose strange songs absorb
mystery, and that is not sailing too far.

   So long…

   P.

Turning from the National Geographic to Peer out the Window

Sometimes
When I hold out my hand,
The habit of winter changes.
I think of it as one of the simple gestures
Guiding the sun:
A quiet moss
Or Astrakhan with its young lambs.
Often
Winter is only one of Poe's stories anyway;
And the drastic nature
Of sudden, subtle changes is everywhere.
At first I am afraid
Of the impulses laws have.
I remember being in the middle of the lake
When the storm came
(*And the storms always come*)
I guess you can say I am afraid
(*I am afraid*)
… of the wind first.
It is ethereal like shade
And silence and sleep.
I remember
The first time I heard the wind
Beat down the lawn, and ever since
I have been too shocked
To stand in the tall grass.
It may not be nice of me
But I cannot forgive that outpouring
Of need the living have
That hurts things.
(*And surely, the wind lives*)

And when I see the things it hurts
I am afraid of the things I hurt.
But I have learned to think
Of the young lambs of Astrakhan,
And how after all
Winter is just one of us
(*Or most likely vis-à-vis*)
And that sometimes
We must despise the law cruelly,
And walk off-course to find ourselves,
And that this change with its violence
Is a kiss.

Sometimes
When I hold out my hand
And the habit of winter changes
I cry for joy.

Lyric 10

Limbs swing out into friendship.
It is a tender day
They cannot touch.
They become frantic
And begin subtle dances.
They dance the dance of pain
For the rain clouds gathered.
They dance the dance of hush
In intervals
For pure blue days
That are like long exotic names.

What would you say woman
If I told you I hoped it would happen,
That I am the son of Kinyanju
Called Kimotho,
That we reach out to certain places
But they are unknown.
They are like strong beasts
These dances.
These beautiful dances
Shared by everybody
As though they are meals.
Or
They are like visiting friends
Serious ones
(By the way, kiss me)
Who run up from the road
To meet you.

If they come together
These dancers
These beautiful branches
I will be right here to meet you.

Lyric 11

There is a woman
Who holds on to my sleep for me.
She is a great blue heron
Strumming the water
For all the little breaths
That support us.

Lyric 12

I believe in myself slowly.
It takes all of the doubt I've got.
It takes my wonder.

VI

*"For many persons, accuracy, or
closeness of resemblance to what is
represented in life, is the principle
means of determining the
excellence of a work of art.*

*"A truthful visual account
can generate its own peculiar
sense of mystery."*

25 Exposures

1   What makes our pictures:
    The darkness inside
    Or the brief light?

2   Here is a tunnel.
    It is a woman's face,
    But the light is not dimming.

3   She said, "I am a dancer."
    Even the camera
    Believed her.

4   It is not cold —
    But their faces are like iron,
    Their hands like cords of wood.

5   The more you walk
    The later it gets.
    You must decide:
    You love her; you love her not.

6   When you retired
    You were going to be rich.
    You had time; you had time.
    Now you have your hands
    On your chin —
    Your oak cane
    On the stove.

7   The skyline is dark.
    We call it evening —
    We know better.

8   They pay you to think.
They pay her to dance –
There is a difference.

9   Your kite's in a tree;
You don't know it.
Your life's on a limb;
You don't know that either.

10   They have discovered their backs.
They have discovered friends can't see everything.

11   It's all in the light:
Your mustache
One eye –
What I cannot see
Makes the picture.

12   Like Spider-Man
You wash windows.
Like Spider-Man
It is all comic –
To depend on a thin line
To work hard
And have doubts.

13   Shutter speed can block a pass.
Shutter speed can show
You are not angry
And for an instant
Hung in the air
You are perfect.

14   You are perfectly trained
      Line or no line
      You charge.

15   The card room is open.
      The man sitting alone at the wall
      Is closed –
      There are limits to everything.

16   You are at the well.
      You have dropped the bucket…
      All the way down
      You feel your child.

17   Cards:
      Jack high, showing
      Undershirt, showing
      Jim Beam, empty
      Showing
      Eyes, red, showing
      You won't let them know,
      Showing
      Time itself,
      Showing.

18   Fire –
      The greatest fear
      Losing everything.

19   You are sitting down.
      She comes in.
      You chew a toothpick
      To her bones.
      She thinks you do not love her.

LOVE IS NOT A CONSOLATION; IT IS A LIGHT

Fool!
You know nothing.

20   The clouds could not live.
There is no f-stop
For real things.

21   I hold on to all these stars
Like small stones.
They are a sign of forgiveness.

22   Absence happens deeply.
It is a radiance
At the end of relationship.
You tell the film you're hungry
And it eats you.

23   She put on her shoes
In a tiny darkness
But he lit a match
And found her.

24   This is how she went about it –
Telling stories in his ear
To please the gods
To make sure the rains came.

25   I realize how happiness
Suddenly clicks
Then endures silence.

Lyric 13

With emotion
The wind holds out its empty hands.
Let's stop all this; let's stop.

The dry grass stands up
In the dust it must learn to live with
And laughs and laughs.

Such tormented lovers
Have at last found trust.
And I wonder this morning

Outside near the edge of everything
Was I really awake when I saw this.

Lyric 14

You take this earth we live on;
You take her
In your empty hands.

You are the washing river
That loves her.

Take off her clothes.

Now:
Where does she come from?
What does she dream of?
What have you learned to say to each other?

VII

*"Light represents the cleanliness
of a spirit which has been
scrubbed by the effects
of endless moral reflection."*

Ocean of the Streams of Story

It is Thursday, October 23.
You like Thursday;
Your baby was born
On the same day as your mother.
You are all tied together in a jaw.
I was thinking how you always notice
The first bit of brown breath
That reaches the grass.

Do you notice me?

Obviously
This writing has its own desire;
I can see it reaching for your hands.
And on this strange Thursday
Beginning to feel cold enough for more blankets
I will ask you to marry me...

Marry me.

But you have not read this yet
And are not as surprised as I am,
Out back digging this pit
And trying to turn the weeds black,
That I think it is time to marry again—
To join our hands
Like the indelible seasons,
Yours white and mine black.
For I have finally come to believe
In our own inner necessities as they are,
Our own Scheherazades
And the ocean of our streams of story

That has made us join our hearts
So we are
Not lost after all as I thought.

Love Poem 4

This is the way
I thought fruit should taste –
Very warm,
And this is the way
I thought it would be in your heart.

Love Poem 6

If I thought of the zucchini bread
Baby
Before I thought of you,
May God strike me dead
Many years from now
When we have crumbled.

DREAMER

I

"Mi wan' opodron
Lek friman Borgu. "

(I want the drumming in the open

Like a citizen who is free.)

*"Fictive kinship ties probably resulted from
relationships among those who had been
on board slave ships together from West Africa."*

We came to know each other
Through the constant touch of our bodies,
The endless devotion
Of our mingled sweat;
Finally I said,
"You stink," in my language.
"Yoruba man, son of a Lagos beast,
So do you," he said
In his own language.
Almighty God, Olofin-Orun,
Discerner of hearts,
I did not kill him;
It was good to know
He too was still human,
For we have come to live
In the enormous hole
Of a world that creaks,
That rocks from side to side
Like the astonishing breast
Of the full moon.
A world fertile with death,
Seductive with madness,
With enough pain to produce crops;
And in this world
We have become as rancid
As salt fish after an enormous journey,
Rancid
With stories of enigmatic love
And profuse loss –
So Olorun
It was because we sensed

We were some last precious gift
For some lost future kin,
It was in that spirit
Wattled and daubed in our own shit
That we reached into the darkness
And became brothers.

*"In certain cases the ties may have
been more than 'fictive,' since individual
cargoes certainly included captives from
common regions, villages and even families…"*

That day
The sun was especially hot;
I want to caution you
It may have unraveled my mind.
That day a Limba woman jumped.
"No matter what others believe," she said,
"I trust my own wisdom
And choose the enduring sea."
I too was at the edge;
A stench was upon us
As thick as soup.
The day before that
I was put down beside her
With the treacherous Wolof.
She had a thick crust of blood
Around her thighs,
Trickles of blood down her legs,
I admit she stank,
I wanted to dream my way into it.
I wanted to dream my way into it
Like gourds of cold seawater,
I wanted to seep my way
Into her darkness,
For ever since we were children
She has been as black
As the river at night to me.
We are from the same village;
Her father, chief.
She has been taught to ignore me;
She is so damn beautiful

And good at it
So damn beautiful
So quiet and peacefully black
And aloof
Beside her I am but a stalk
Of dry grass in the harmattan.
That day
When they took us up on deck,
We all crumpled in the light
Spoke to ourselves
With the same crisp mockery
Of the snapping sails,
But not her.
I would have done anything
To clean her body.
Killed a hundred Wolof,
Turned into tears.
Swelled into a water gourd.
Transformed myself into goats
Or pigs and licked or chewed –
For love is neither slavery
Nor grace nor cleanliness,
But an immense fire at the hearth
A tribal sacrifice
A curious self-revelation
A lusty redemption
An unconditional desire
To be swept up with somebody
Into something else.
Someday
Before we are through in this house
From which I am afraid
We will never walk out alive,
I want to be shackled to her,
I want us to speak to each other
With the whole mouth.

"There are two ways of looking at African
Negro sculpture that, for fifty years, have impeded
a true understanding of that art. One
is the notion that an African carving or casting
is 'pure art' and that its quality can be
fully possessed by European aesthetic standards,
without reference to the culture in and for
which it was made, the other and opposite
view sees in an example of Negro sculpture not
a work of art but merely a primitive utilitarian
object made by a tradition-fettered artisan
for a barbarous community devoid of aesthetic
feeling of any kind."

When the butterflies appear
The tilling of the fields begins.
We dance like shrill sounds
As light as we can
For creatures without wings
To the "do" spirits,
Looking at the world
Through the veil of our painted masks
And braided ropes,
Hoping to imbue in ourselves
What we know in the soft earth
Is truly divine.

"… In 1934 no fewer than seven hundred and sixty-five stones [figures] and heads were discovered in a clearing… in a majority of these carvings the features are sufficiently individualized for them to be considered as portraits."

Today
I am working on the head of Osisi
The ambitious woman.

> *My head—which is wearing*
> *a bright scarf today—*
> *will surely give me*
> *male and female children.*

It is as though I am working
On a silk-cotton tree
In the forest.
Or an eagle in the sky.
Ambition, like death,
Is so demanding—
A little bush becomes a court case—
Yet
When I put my chisel in her face
I look for her in vain,
I must consult the oracle
To make the stone pregnant.

Keba,
A man of middle age,
Of sweet belly laughter,
Will be next.
People
Cannot run away from him.
He has a heart
The size of the chief's house.

I must keep the calabash
Full with wine
And the sun at his back.

Had I known my destination
Was to reach for heaven
From earth
Through the indelible lines
And curves
Of what we are thinking
And who we are,
I would have asked
To be like the unanointed men
Who leave their lives behind
Like the birds
While their bodies take them
To other limbs.
But what I am ordained to do
Is a hunter's song,
An Ijala.

"For all this, however, we must still face the
fact that our knowledge of the background of
African art is elementary. And while we keep
in mind the vital importance of enriching,
whenever possible, the communication of a piece
of Negro sculpture through the marriage of
ethnographic and aesthetic considerations, we
should not quixotically deny ourselves the
aesthetic gratification which art is able
to provide each new generation of observers,
foreign as that gratification may be to the
essential character and message of Negro art."

I think I will make the man thin
Like my cousin Yerema
With the long neck.
He is one's self
In one's own right,
A strong dark wood
As distinguishable from others
As a Muhammadan's sermon.
It will take three days
To sharpen my wits
And rough out the body.
I think I will make Zala
The woman.
She alone has the lips
Of early morning;
The enormous ability to fill and rise,
To gird herself in the loincloth
Of your deepest thoughts
And understand them –
For this sculpture will be
The undergarment
For a couple in love,

And if you cut off
Any piece of it,
That piece will also grow.
And I will tell the wood
To tell the man inside
Kneel down on the ground
By his yams,
Then arch his back
And extend his long neck,
His face looking behind him.
And I will tell the wood
To tell the woman
Standing up behind him
To bend down
And kiss his lips,
Zala's breast,
O Zala
The perfect headrest.
And this pose
Will almost be a complete circle
Without hesitation or fear,
Not a place for a jealous man
Or an oppressed woman.
And the tension will be
Gentle and firm,
Held together by hunger
And appetite,
By chance and wisdom.
And you will see
How their loins burn –
After all who can escape
The small bearded gods
We worship…

This will be a piece that comes alive
And serves when lovers weep at night.

"On the northern shore of the Gulf of Guinea
especially in the Gold Coast and Ivory Coast, we
find a curious expression of lyric fantasy in
small bronzes produced by the cire perdue
method and used by the natives for weighing
gold dust."

I told her to go outside,
Little girl
Who is the younger of twins,
And look carefully
At the small yellow birds
And to learn how to speak
With understanding of another,
For in this world
It is too easy to be a slave…

This was to be only a small piece
To weigh gold,
But later that afternoon
When she left
I also started to cut
The story into a large stone.
Of all that I saw them do
Only this song will be left out:

"I shall return no more, I shall return no more
my [mother]."

I was to become a Bajan.
I did not know that;
I am a Wolof
Captured at the hooves of my prey.
My name means
Fruit, seed, kernel.
I am my mother's
Youngest child;
I have never seen her again.
Never seen her mash or kneed
Or dip into the water again
To splash my face.
She was blunt,
And as stubborn as the beard
I hate to shave.
She was so beautiful
The village thought she was cursed.
She was so imperfect and warm
In her thoughts like an old fire.
Before I left I heard her say:

We call the dead—they answer.
We call the living—they do not.

*"We judge a work of art by its effect on
our sincere and vital emotion, and nothing
else. All this critical twiddle-twaddle
about style and form, all this pseudo-
scientific classifying and analyzing of books
in an imitation-botanical fashion, is
mere impertinence and mostly dull jargon."*

What do stories do?
Affect us,
Nothing else.
If that is scientific, fine;
If that is not, tough "T,"
Twiddle-twaddle
And all that rot.
My response to the story
About the pig being slaughtered
Was like the eleven-year-old's.
"It made me sick."
Especially that part
When the knife dove into the throat,
Splash.
My legs went to jelly.
My head to peanut butter.
I thought it was cruel,
But I was moved
Like the blood gushing down,
To understand the need for food,
The need for trade
And the need to make families
Slaves.
Who was I to intervene or recoil
From the story?
It made me furious.
I kept thinking of all the blood

In the bucket
That holds names:
Akam — The small
Remnant of a once mighty people,
Sekyere with the capital
Dwaben to the east,
Kumase — a town,
Krobò — a mountain country.
I began to think of the dance
Asáw
In the blood,
The kindness — *ayam yé,*
Our sins and our worth,
The blood all over the language.
Osékám twá adé.
(A knife cuts.)
Okromfó wi áde.
(A thief steals.)
Owo ka onípa.
(A serpent bites.)
In a story, I get involved.
I try to make the last page last.
I rivet myself to the names:
Kwasi, Abene, Benada.
Kofi, Ata — a twin.
She always went there;
She was always told
Not to go.
Whereas I was blind,
Now I see
The blood in our language.
Mepe hó mmòn sènhá.
(I like that place better than this.)
(I shall be able to match
Or to overcome him.)

Metumi no.
(He is unequal to the business.)
Otumí sa yò.
I am astonished,
Shocked,
I shudder at this story.
Boys were suddenly changed into fathers;
Fathers weeping became sons.
My head aches
As if the smith is still
Hammering iron,
Or the women giving birth.
I know
Like the pig in the story
People uttered groans,
The eloquent delivered speeches,
The militants foamed.
The earth produces food
In this story—
Lots of food...
Whereas I was blind,
Now I can see.
A knife cuts.
A thief steals.

But reader,
What about you?

II

"As I said earlier, in imposing a conception on events, all human individuals create the 'reality' to which they respond."

Dreamer

1   There are few probabilities through
Which dreamers do not pass...

The first dream
Is the bright red dream
Of our mother's heart.
It is her sacrifice
Of something eternal
In herself, for us.
The Arabs say
Blood has flowed
Let us begin again.

The heart is like a cup, or a coffer,
or a cave. It holds the image of the
sun within us. It is a center of illumination
and happiness and wisdom. To dream
of the heart is always to dream of
the importance of love...

The second dream is the inauguration
Of the soul. In this dream we are
Confronted by a host of birds...

Some were guileless
Like the doves,
Said Odo of Tusculum,
Cunning
Like the partridges.
Some came to the hand
Like the hawks.
Others fled from it
Like the hens,

Some enjoyed the company
Of people
Like swallows,
Others preferred solitude
Like the turtledoves,
But all eventually flew away.

"Living is not necessary, but navigation
is," said Pompey the Great.

B. 1725, London
Mother devout as gunpowder
Seemingly clairvoyant
Taught her only child
To read by four
Arithmetic and Latin by six
Dies when he is seven.

I am dreaming
I am in the dark
And it is raining
And she is the rain.

To dream that you are in the dark
is a sign of difficulties ahead; if
you fall or hurt yourself you can expect
a change for the worse, but if you
succeed in groping to the light, that
is another matter...

Father, master of ships,
Lively in the Mediterranean trade,
Unusual qualities –
Educated in Spain, stern.

I listen to nothing
But the silence
Of my father; the dream
Says
He is the rudder
And the compass.

If, in your dreams, you see your
father and he speaks to you, it is
a sign of coming happiness. If he is
silent, or if he appears to be ill or
dead, then you may expect trouble...

Sent to sea at ten,
Acted like a verb in disagreement,
Of course
Bright,
But no eagle—
A mess.

I have vague
Dreams now
Of intelligent flowers.
I cannot say
If their roots
Are in the ground
Or in the air.

By seventeen
A wildflower
In the field of Jesus.
Pious, books, fasting,
Abstinence from meat,
A canon in his meditation
And silence,

But like the weeds
Loved to curse.

Flowers, one of nature's best dreams.
This foretells great happiness, unless
you throw away the blossoms…

1742
A lot more flexible,
Falls in love,
Misses his ship,
A freethinker now,
Less of a thorn
In the side of God.

I dream that I
Am always with her,
A freckle on her wrist,
A flower in her hair,
A ridiculous flying fish –
Sliced
And dressed
And set on the table.

As I told you before,
He missed his ship,
Became a lover
Rather than a Jamaican
Planter,
Father as expected
Furious.

Love is a dream of contraries as far
as sweethearts are concerned. To dream
that you do not succeed in love is a

sign that you will marry and have
a happy life. To dream that you are in
the company of your lover is also fortunate...

Late 1743
Kidnapped into the Navy
(What else)
Coming from Mary's house.
Taken from his own life,
Focused into new pieces.

I dream about my fortune,
A fragrance captured
In a jar,
A freckle without a wrist,
A wisp
Foxlike at the edge
Of the wind.

Fortune is a dream of contraries: the more
fortunate and successful you are in imagination,
the greater will be your real struggles...

How do we fit together
When we are not free?
What kind of animal are we?
How many heads do we have?
How many tails?
The sea
Is a strange piece of property
On which to discuss this,

On the HMS *Hardwick*
One month later
Midshipman John Newton:

I have eaten war
Like a cluster
Of delicious fruit.
The ironic juices
Running from my lips
That was my dream.

The reality of war is the dream of it. Beware
of those things that appear so friendly
but have no reason...

1774
The *Hardwick*
Ordered to the East Indies.
First our hero visits Mary again.
(You're wrong)
Almost misses ship,
Completely misses the point.
Given small boat of men
To go ashore at Plymouth,
Deserts.

My dreams here
Were father, compass,
Fog, leakage,
And ultimately, learning,
With us
Like our laundry.

We are always pulling from our past. Fossils
are the dream of the sickness of someone
you have not met for a long time. When
this happens brew herbs, add honey
and lemon, sip and inhale deeply...

Captured like a frog,
Returned, put in irons,
Stripped, flogged, degraded,
Returned to foremast.

This is that point many people would
call a black moment, an unfortunate
color on things. I will not do that. For
black is a contrary at funerals and our
hero has just died a little as we
all tend to from time to time. And even
though that is true I will not do
that either. I will not talk of the great
white moment of death, I will not talk
of the great blue and purple moments
in the prosperity of pain. I will not
talk of the great red or scarlet moments
of quarrels and loss of friends, or
the crimson pleasure of the unexpected,
the mental tints of yellow and orange
that show you should always expect
change, or the feeling of knowing green
because you have been on a long journey.
All the colors are conjurers when our
mysteries are being solved. And if this could
not be his dream then by now it should
be ours…

We are not holy
The wind says in the sails
As he works.
It has never been otherwise
Though we live in the most
Devout of stories like litmus paper
Constantly changing color

Just to prove something
Is happening.

The sadness in his dream is a good omen
for the future. It is a quest for lasting joy,
and so is punishment a dream of unexpected
pleasure…

Works quietly for weeks.
His silence
Darns a temperate
Healing thread.
His eyes
Become an elaborate
Decorative art
Avoiding everyone.

"Every month," said Cicero
"the moon contemplates
its trajectory
and the shrubs
and animals grow."

He has done to himself
What is easy.
He must now blossom
Out of his new secrets
Even if joy is ephemeral.

Suddenly
He begins to sing,
Creates songs about fish
And clouds.

Fish are a dream of penetrative motion,
clouds are a dream of appearances always
in a state of change…

We must be patient
With the overfecundity
Of his youth.
We must let him
Climb and descend the mast
Like a weapon.
Trade him
To a slaver's ship
To subdue the threat
To discipline
In his strangely awakening
Joy.
We must let him
Choose his monsters
And the myths
Of his own worth –
The enemy always being
The forces threatening
From within.

Paul said, "We wrestle not against flesh
and blood, but against principalities, against
powers, against the rulers of the darkness
of this world, against spiritual wickedness in
high places…"

Suddenly,
Begins to breathe
Different songs
In his six-months' stay
Along the Sierra Leone coast.

Troublesome songs,
Songs of quick wit
And devastating rhymes
Ridiculing ship's officers,
Crew loves them,
Becomes a choir.

To dream that you hear other people
singing shows that the difficulties
that will come for you will come through
your dealings with other people...

The irate mate
Assuming command
After the death of the captain
Threatens
To put Newton
On a man-o'-war.

The Royal Navy is not an obstacle dream;
it is an elaborate exhibition of the
nuances of living death...
Occupation: slave dealer
Place: Sierra Leone
On one of the Plantanes
Features: Short, white male
Name: Clow
Other information: Black wife
Name: sounds like P.I.

John Newton
Bargains his life
Into this extravagant story.
He will become a slave
Because P.I. will hate him.

He will become ill
With fever.
He will be denied
Food,
Denied water,
Tormented by Black slaves
On command,
Put to work
On a lime tree plantation
Enjoying only the scents
And dreaming
Of his earthly desires,
Will master the six books
Of Euclid,
Drawing the diagrams
With a long stick
In the wet sand.

Six is, like *two,* a particularly ambiguous
number to dream about, but it
establishes equilibrium. It unifies
the triangles of fire and water and
symbolizes the human soul. Six is
the hermaphrodite, a personality integrated
despite its duality.

If this is a story
Of the reasoning of slavery,
Where are we?
What have we been doing
To people,
To the light
From which life emanates?

Slavery is a story
Of procreation,
Of magic religious thinking,
Of the androgynous divinity
Within us.

No story can be this happy
Unless it is married
To something deeply within us.
It is not *them*
Who have done it to *us,*
Or *us*
Who have done it to *them.*
It is the antagonistic dream
Of unreconciled love.

To dream of erotic love is to dream of
the desire to die in the object of desire, to
dissolve in that which is already
dissolved. The Book of Baruch says erotic
desire and its satisfaction is the key
to the origin of the world. Disappointment
in love and the revenge which follows
in its wake are the roots of all the evil
and selfishness in the world. The whole
of history is the work of love.

2   "The character of the image," said Shukrâshârya,
"is determined by the relationship between
the worshiper and the worshiped."

On the beach,
He eats the fruit
Of his own way;
He fills himself
With his own devices;

He continues to draw
In the sand.

Each grain
Is a small,
Precise form
Of salvation
That has occurred,
A god come to earth
In another form,
A private,
Innate sacrifice.
Providence does not tire.
We are ready to go on
With the story.

It has come to this:
When his father dreams
He only sees
The broad face
Of sadness,
The soft grassland
Where only asphodels grow,
And the idea of water
Expanding into tears.

But to dream of sadness is a good
omen, a transposition of suffering to the
spiritual: this dream is like an herb,
a seasoning, a bitter root, medicinal,
something poisonous, but nevertheless
something that eventually withers away.

When you
Come on to squally weather,

When the wind
Is about SW,
When
You sway up the yard
Fix the trysail,
Put people to making
Sennit and swab,
Ask for my son.
Ask the *Lamb*,
The *Beverly*, the *Golden Lyon*,
Ask Job Lewis,
Have you seen my boy?
Have you seen my boy?

One thousand years before Christ, Solomon
said that the way of a ship in the midst
of the sea was too wonderful for him
to understand.

Meanwhile,
Clow: shamed
Into freeing his fellow
White man.
After all
They share the same hair,
The same instinctual life,
The same irrational power.
There is no victim here:
This is a story of love's
Sadness,
Of the spirit of love's ferocity
And savage insensibility,
And the name of Jesus
Turned in hymns,
Spewed into the fringes

Of the forest,
Spewed on the deep blue sea.

What dream is this, is that what you said?
My God, this is the dream of the dragon,
the fabulous animal, the amalgam of
aggression, the serpent, the crocodile, the
lion, what we like to think is the
antediluvian nature of love.

John is free now.
John is free to slave,
Free to be reluctant,
To give up profit
and return home.

Ask the master of the *Greyhound.*
Have you seen my boy?
Have you seen my boy?

To find money in your dream is not fortunate
at all. There will be some sudden advancement
or success, but it will prove
disappointing. Reader, remember this
statement by Virgil, "It will be pleasant
to remember these things hereafter."

You cannot blame
The sea on a woman.
Unlike the seasons
It has no ribs
Though
It has a crown,
Wears a sheath,
Swings a sickle,

Adores the sun,
And is known
As bareheaded and leafless.
The sea is the emblem
Of the great capricious world;
The naked image of flux
Vibrating between life and death.

There is a dream called "Dire is the tossing
deep the groans; come let us heel, list
and stoop." And when John heard this
on his way home, it was as if he
had read 2 Kings 10:16, "Come with me
[brother] and see my zeal for the lord."

For twelve months
The *Greyhound*
Sought gold,
Ivory, dyer's wood,
Beeswax,
And Newton sought the Lord.

The way of a ship in the midst of the sea
is too wonderful to understand.

Youth is not innocence.
It is not a militant puzzlement.
It is a methodological initiation
Into the ubiquitous life
Of sin.
For a life without sin
Is no life at all.
And so he wanders on
Like Paul,
So very Christian about it,

At once wretched and delivered.
Thinking with his mind
He is serving God,
But with his flesh
The law of sin.

Call out John Newton.
Call out
To Joshua, Ruth,
Samuel, Obadiah,
Esther, Zechariah,
Luke and Timothy.
The world
Is a masterfully round
Secret
That embraces everything,
And it is time
To reach into the horizon,
Now.
It is time to choose
Your ship,
And the triangle of your life
Upon the salty sea.

As you can see, dreams are without reason,
without solution, without proof, the
unedited version of our love, our aspiration,
our hurt... Call out John Newton. Call out...

Back home
Offered captaincy of ship.
Refuses.
Sails as first mate
On the *Brownlow*.

Collects slaves.
Takes them to South Carolina.

He begins the dream of questions: "What
was the mode used in stowing the slaves
in their apartments?"

Returns home,
Marries Mary Cattlett,
Assumes first command,
The *Duke of Argyle,*
140 tons burthen.

Marriage is the dream of sulfur and
mercury. Some believe it is a most fortunate
omen, a volatile conciliation, a fragile
union. They are right. It is one of the great
uncharted seas of individuation. It is
said, "If you are separated from your
opposite you consume yourself away..."

Dead reckoning
Magnetical Amplitude   W° 25.30N°
True Amplitude   W° 6.30°
Variation   19° in Western
Lattitude per Account   50° 48^m

One-third of the slaves will die
In middle passage
Some say fifty million
Started the trip
Some say fifteen.

The dream of questions is a bright necklace
with two ornáments on it: liberty and
love, not truth.

"At noon some small rain...
Had an indifferent observation..."

"We take the two men-boys
For some shallop rigging,
We do not take
The two fallen-breasted women..."

"Dear Mary,
        Today, saw
        My quondam Black
        Mistress P.I. –
        I believe
        I made her sorry
        For her former ill
        Treatment of me."

The trouble with atonement is it is like
a sphinx, several parts human, several
parts bull, dog, lion, dragon, or bird.
When we are dreaming of atonement, no
matter how subtly, we must remember
we are not dreaming of a verb.

"I watch them work
The tie, tacklc,
And lower lift.
The boatswain
Speaks to Bredson
About the score
In one of the strops.

Thomas Creed
Sits with his splicing fids;
Tucks the strands
Of the tack cringle.
His fingers are either
Little mystics or snakes."

When you dream the dream of square-sail
rigging you are dreaming the dream
that the same side is always before
the wind. At the dawn of Swedish history
it was believed Erik Vädderhatt, the
King of the Svear, could turn the wind
and cruise endlessly. Ships are supposed
to be emblems of transcendental joy…

"Do the male slaves
Ever dance
Under these circumstances?"

"After every meal
They are made to jump
In their irons;
But I cannot call it dancing."

"What is the term
That is usually given to it?"

"It is by the slave dealers
Called dancing."

"Unclewed the sails.
They too in their shackles
Danced in the wind."

"Dear Mary,
        I watched the land wind
        Do to the sails
        What it does
        To our hair.
        I dreamed of dancing
        With you
        Into the cold water,
        Our wet clothes
        Like nets and entanglements
        Around our desire."

They would call them up
Two by two, equivocal,
Unmasked,
Making it possible
To be classified
Forever:
Pairs of birds,
Pairs of oxen,
Pairs of sheep,
Reptiles, lions,
Elephants, antediluvian,
Carnivorous, herbivorous,
Fabulous, beautiful,
Ugly, strange,
Cocks, locusts, bears,
Foxes, and even flies,
All of them black;
All of them in colonnade
To the gates of hell.

John did baptize
In the wilderness,
Did call out to Judæa

And Jerusalem
Come lay down
Your life
In the River Jordan,
Participate in his death
And his resurrection.

They said
They were refreshing them,
But the shackles still clanged,
And most of them still stank,
And many finding holes
In the netting
Jumped overboard
And baptized themselves
Bobbing in the adoring
Loins of the sea.

"Dear Mary,
          The three greatest blessings
          Of which human nature is capable
          Are undoubtedly religion,
          Liberty and love."

The shape of a ship's hull is determined by
the materials, methods of construction,
means of propulsion, use, fashion, and
whim. This is a dream of law and
the minute verities of justice, the eighth
enigma of the tarot.

First part fair,
The latter cloudy,
Winds becoming unusual,
Clouds dark, great lightning...

I think of what we've done,
My own illumination
Before it is too late:

The palm and needle whippings,
The short splice,
Blackwall hitches,
Sheet bends.

Quickly rummage
The rigging details,
The yardarm blocks,
The tackles.

Recall work
On the pintles,
The rudder head.

Have Billinge
Check barricado and stores,
Especially powder and slaves.

On this day
Of the second voyage
Of *The African*, 1754,
Weighed,
Bound by God's permission
To St. Christophers,
We are ready for our justice,
To be winnowed like barley
On the threshing floor.

The great dream of the dark, with the
lonely extroverted lamp, the intuitive ship,
and the wind tossing on the innovative sea

should moor somewhere. "Why is this
so?" asked Kuo Hsi. For in our landscapes
and our seascapes are the personalized items
of our consciousness, the coarse grist
of our imagination, the flirtatious metaphors
stirring our ethics, and the boldly stroked
delineations of our unraveling possibilities
and original nature.

Through the night
We were played with
Like kittens.
The slaves spilled
Out nightmares of themselves
And groans.
We will all
Need dawn's shawl
This morning.
I hope
She is good to us.

Osiris was slain by Set and put
together again by Isis. John will dream
like this, off and on, and then quit the
sea. This is his last voyage. He will
lose no slaves and no crew, and it will
be called a blessing. At a time like
this the Egyptians would build a
monolith to marry the enigmatic tension
between life and death. John will
change his dreams, now, from the menstrual
dreams of the slaver to the menthol dreams
of the minister. Showing the devastating evil
we do, like a storm, is only a stepping-

stone to something else.
Sing brother.

I will become sermons,
He says,
That understand what I've done.
Sing
I will become hymns
Bound in the skin
Of what I've done.
I will be patient with Cowper,
Inspiring to Wilberforce
        And Wordsworth;
I will attract the awakened crowds,
The abolitionist.
I will stand at the altar.
Sing brother
Dressed in black,
Testifying,
Testifying...

I dream I will not be forgiving him
for the timeliness of his innocence, for
betrothing the dead to the dead,
but will be lifting
up my hands to an appetite for life
that will take slavers and slaves with me.

I wish
There was no timelessness,
That slavery was over
And so far away
It was an incredibly mysterious
Jungle –
Somewhere else.

An uncharted river
Canopied by extensive moss –
Somewhere else.
A spectacular ragged
Waterfall
Mystically expressed
Over an enormous
Obsidian wall,
But it is *right here*
In my pouch, today,
Like the acori beads
I have been swimming with
For hours –
Presidential, prime ministerial,
Corporate, grassroots based.
Right here,
Racist, imperial, and sexist.
Right here,
Woefully spendthrift
And Democratic,
Anally retentive
And Republican,
Militantly inappropriate,
And so good to itself
That it jogs.

III

"Monkey say wha' in him mout,
no fe him, but wha' in him belly
a fe him."

(What is in my cheek is not mine,
but what has gone into my belly,
that is my very own.)

That in Itself Is the Proverb

Tonight
The old man sits outside the shack—
Buckpot moon, bad,
Unconscious,
Long unwithered hair
Shaking on the sea like dreadlocks.
He is quiet, unlike Babylon.
Quiet as the small gazelle
Or the strong, brutal leopard,
And black enough,
That in itself is the proverb.
Indeed, I hear the sea
Cus' at Bottom Bay
Say *phhh,* say *phhhh*
A little more human than before.
Phhh and *cus'.*

Gazelle man, quiet,
Laid back like Jah.
Obviously, he loves she;
Secretly, he adores she butt –
Phhhh, phhh, and *cus', cus'*
In Babylon.

I think, he would give her bare bananas
For her blue dress,
And behave in the spume about she
Like you have to grieve before you walk,
Like you have to mumble before you talk.
Old man, Egret...
Know she lips brackish
Know she eyes merely manchineels,

Know she against the cliffs,
Cus', cus' and *phhhh.*

For a moment,
Caught up in your ethereal value
Not to move but to be,
I, too, feel old enough
To understand the sea.

Sunday

Today,
The sea has its own religion;
It is as blue
As an acori bead
I rubbed in my hand.

I think
Of swimming out
   for miles
     and miles
       in prayer.

I think
Of never struggling back
In doubt.

As though
In a world like this
Love starts over and over again.

We Are Going to Be Here Now

I wanted to start the story
In the hedgerow
At the side of the road
Like the khus-khus grass.
You can be anyone you please.
If I can be Mr. Tambo.
Dig me out of the ground;
Hang me up
And when I'm dry
And fragrant,
And you're still wet,
You'll see that I can't
Live without you, baby,
My fishtail palm,
My cane,
My rondeletia.
And even in our games,
Hemped and flaxed in the imagination,
I believe you
Like I believe Olaudah Equiano,
Completely,
Tone and all,
And any of us who have been stolen
And run away from the subscriber
With a cloth jacket
Or a thin dress.
Run into the hills to become cattle
Or horses, cimarróned,
And finally free –
Animals again.
God, I believe you history
Because your touch is a shore
Against the southern equatorial currents

Behind us,
And we are here now.
And at night when you embrace me
I know it is Antigua
Because Suriname is mortally ill –
Toal stand is doodstyk krankon.
We are going to be here now.
Here in the trusted word of the ground cover,
The worm weed
Used in the ritual bath after childbirth.
Here in the juice of the Spanish needle
For our blind inflamed eyes.
We are going to be nivway,
And paw paw, and duppy gum
Until our nails become the arrowheads
Of our profound loss,
And we offer them up again,
This time not as God and Gold
But as Race and Gender
Until we finally create America.

Lord, Man

You pick a basket of bean;
"God," you say,
When you mouth wide open
I see the wonderful round world.
I say, "Lord, maan, you a beast,
You a beast."
I begin to feel my feet turn hoof.
You mouth, wooman,
Turn sea grape, gully plum, dunks.
Hair on my arms turn weeds
Of the field:
Duckweed, sour grass, pussley,
From now on *burning mouth vine.*
Whatever we do or say
Will smell like breath of earth,
Will be the soul giver of children,
Will curve like a weapon
Into terrible scars;
            I know
I will love you like a war,
And repent like medicine,
Almighty God, Imana,
The one who plans,
The protector of possessions,
Release me from your arms, now.
Never save me,
Let me love like thunder,
Let me grieve like famine,
Let me hurt her like I hurt the forest,
Let there be days
When it is wished all men were dead,

Because I done been through this already,
Because I done been through this already,
And it won't save the poem.

Tale

Cat gone down the road.

What she name, girl?
Jane (cat).

What happen to cat's tongue
I ask.
I got it she say.

What you name?
Jane, too.

You know what happen Jane (girl)
When you got cat's tongue?
No.

The language change.

You see it (language)
Put its belly down and yawn.

That yawn makes the verbs quiver
Like cocks of lightning,
And lightning is a sign you know.
It can put a hole in the ground.

The mother of pots is a hole in the ground.
The mother of people is God.
The mother of language is that cat's tongue.

Tongue is a planter like hoe,
a silence like seed,
a consort like water.

What you say you name again?
Jane.
You gonna be busy girl.

Once

Once I went hunting in the bush
Of the human skull.

To please the people I met,
I gave flesh.

If by chance you happen to find me
And I am at rest,

It is their gift.

Worship

The storm god kneels down
And attends the river.
Men bring their boats in
With the same beat
That pumps their hearts.
When they are finished,
They stand in a huddle
And admire him.
Some think over the years
His hair has grown longer
And so magnificent
For the crowds that provide
The bones, and the blood,
And the breath of his life.

Focus

Riding through the sky
In a new chariot,
Dawn comes
With his ruddy horses,
His mother and his wife.
Rasta maan wades
Into the full force of the sea
With him,
Letting the water meander
In his matted locks
And compose itself into tributaries
As he swims.
Knotty-head maan needs this moment
Of affirmation.
He too is a prince
Spilling out of the darkness.

And as he does so,
I reach for my stout black brother,
My camera.
It is not as heavy as the false,
Or as intricate as loss.
I both focus and forsake,
Focus and forsake,
Like a man freed
From his own death,
Until I know it is right.
So Jah did it
And did not really die,
But went into himself.
And so *Rasta maan* swims off,
Deeply into the God he is praying to.

And as he finally raises his hand
For the catch,

I click.

Talk

He hand on me back
Movin'
Movin'
Like a sentence
Assembling he words.

How he do this
Belong
To the many small bearded mysteries
Of the Lord thy God
Movin' on dis earth.

I know what you are doin'
Maan.
Like the object of the verb,
I feel you slidin' you hand
Down to me backyard
Like you own the whole daam house –

Sayin, *"Woom-an, woom-an*
The night belong to we."

You are a fragrant politician:
Part marvelous *black sage,*
Part spotted *search me heart,*
Part *ganja* in de mind,
Fool,
Part *English lime.*
Barbados, the night belong to we,
Barbados, the beaches belong to we.

I see you
Like I see the natural process
Of weight and height;
A significance movin' beyond me.

You an ol' man ya know;
Got more children
Than you got teet'.
What do you t'ink you gonna do
Wit me?

Yet you holding me
Nice na:
Like a garden *callaloo*,
An *oxeye daisy* or a *hug me close*...

Saying
"Dar-lin', Dar-lin'
Love don't love nobody but you."

Byum, you too *day*, man;
            you too *day*—
And precious,
Love.

When I am in the hands
Of the *Allhambys*
You give me the shirt off you
Back
And the blood in you heart.

You more than a village ram
On a walk;
You a touching man
Who' talk start high

Off the ground in a large tree
And work its way down to the roots.

I use you words like baskets,
Ol' as I am.
I use you patience
Like seasoning on meat.

You know…
Love ain't using nobody,
Nobody but you.

Dread

It is simple, Black man,
You must engage the unconscious.
Rastafari is in you.
The fierce symbol of the lion
Is love.

Dreadlocks, maan,
Knotty dread

It is your stark raving possibility,
It is your discontent,
And you are sanctified.
It is your denied self come closer,
And you are sanctified.
Rebel leader after rebel leader,
You are sanctified.
Slave revolt after slave revolt,
And you are sanctified.

Dreadlocks, maan,
Knotty dread

It is that look in your eyes
When you're traveling back.
It is revival
By bits and pieces of the spirit
Possessed.
It is the pain of the absence
Become presence.
It is Africa.

So Dreadlocks, maan,
Knotty dread,
The fierce symbol of the lion.
Is love.

Pearle's Poem

She sits in the marketplace
Issuing, like a bright star.
The origin of this beauty
Is her print dress,
So wild and deeply moving
It is a fable
By which to live,
To blend into
As if it were a mosaic of water
Coursing through Guyana
To the unreadable sea.
It has the lightning of her heart,
The thundering battles
Of her guilt and pain,
The dense jungles of her unrequited sorrow
Where the bright birds of her hope
Calypso into their ecstasy.

In front of her
Is her biblical bondage
Of yams, breadfruit,
Mangoes and pears,
Each stacked like a separate prayer,
A redeeming angel,
And the triumphant disposition
Of a true saint.
Women like her
Do not cry or laugh in public,
They condense
The antithetical flaws of the world
Into an awakened responsibility of color.
They are not imperialist
With an urgent knowledge;

They are people who doze in impudent hats
Who have remained
The intricately unraveled villagers
Of the themes of rain and sun
And drought
Part earth, part wind
And like my dying mother,
Part fire.

Pentecostal

All night
I kept my loneliness to myself
Like the wind god Amalivaca
Did for many years,
Then folded it up
Into the ends of the morning darkness
In small enough pieces
To blow through my four-hole flute.
I am looking for a circle of dancers
Who touch
By the nature of their unusually
Long shadows;
I am looking for a drumbeat
To accompany
What is a bloodknot of kindness
Between us,
Taken
From the great strength of a healing music,
Taken
From the sanctuary of a singer's open hands
That eventually
Will plait us into strands
Of the everlasting hair
That make up the forgiving rainbow.

Song

Fishermen
Pursue the sea
As if it were
A naked woman.
That is why
They rise early
And leave their wives
And go to boats
To mumble through
All the natural
Gradations of purpose
That are deeply imbued
In the incomprehensible
Pain of living.

Don't get me wrong,
The sea
Does not want them
At all
No matter what it's done,
And that is why
Ahab went mad
When he saw the sea
Is just what it is,
The sea,
And nothing more,
Despite the fine crepe dresses
The wind and sun
Love to wear.
And they in turn
Are not mendacious
At all
For how they behave,

For they are not human
Beings
Facing year after year
With the unwitting limits
Of surreal nets
And traps that work
Like threatening dreams.

They are just
Capricious things
Trying to feel comfortable
At what they do.
And despite all their seductivity,
The fishermen
Are able to find
In the essential qualities
Of the plain deep water itself
That source
For the silence in themselves,
For their ecstatic gasps of joy
And their pruned, unwilling
Sighs of loss.

And if that is not what love is for,
Then what is it?

Carnival

The sun's return is magical;
And once a year, finally
More than we can bear.
That is why, suddenly,
We break out into a sensual
Frenzy of light
And sound
And motion
And color
Plunging ourselves into chaos,
For we are nervous
But we say it is a celebration
As we realize our lives
Have been nothing more
Than a mischief of patterns
And organizations
Against our fear of the capricious –
Like the essence of the trees and caves,
Like the essence of the growing crops,
Like the essence
Of all the herds of animals,
Like the essence of the clan and tribe,
Even our passionate anger,
Even our violence,
Even our cold indifference,
Our clandestine cruelty,
Our gentle warmth,
Our nurturing abundance,
And our generosity
As we struggle with our volatile selves
Trying to become one with the gods.

I

Bajan (p. 120)	A Barbadian – one from Barbados.
harmattan (p. 112)	A hot, dry wind from North Africa.
Ijala (p. 115)	A hunting song – a song that deals with the epic struggles and mythical issues present in the hunt.
Lagos beast (p. 109)	An insulting name for a Yoruba man or woman.
Limba (p. 111)	A West African people.
Olofin-Orun, also Olorun (p. 109)	A Yoruba deity.
Wolof (p. 111)	A West African people, disliked because they helped European slavers raid for slaves.

II

"Dreamer" tells the story of John Newton, Anglican minister, abolitionist, and hymnist, known as the author of "Amazing Grace." He was a slave-ship captain before turning to the ministry. The poem depends on a reading of his ship's journals and some biographical essays.

acori bead (p. 150)	A small blue bead.
Svear (p. 144)	Old Swedish for "Swedes."
Vädderhatt (p. 144)	Literal definition is "weather hat;" infers that he could change the weather, or the direction of the wind simply by turning the direction of the hat on his head.

Allhambys (p. 166)	A family of money lenders in Barbados known for their bizarre and ruthless methods of collecting.
Amalivaca (p. 172)	A South American Indian deity.
buckpot (p. 152)	A small ceramic cooking stove and pot.
callaloo (p. 166)	A wild grass used as greens.
cimarrón (p. 155)	A Spanish word for runaway horses and cattle; later, word becomes *maroon* – a runaway slave living in the hills and forests.
cus' (p. 152)	A contraction of "curse."
dreadlocks (p. 152)	A matted hairstyle worn by Rastafarians.
duckweed, dunks, gully plums, pussley, sea grapes, sour grass (p. 155)	Some fruits and wild grasses.
duppy gum, nivway, paw paw (p. 156)	Native West Indian plants.
Olaudah Equiano (p. 155)	An eighteenth-century African who wrote one of the earliest known slave autobiographies.
Imana (p. 157)	An African deity.
Jah (p. 152)	God.
khus-khus grass (p. 155)	The hedgerow grass that grows along the end of a sugarcane field – tall and thick.
knotty-head (p. 163)	Reference to Rastafarian dreadlocks.

manchineel (p. 152)	A tree – its fruits are poisonous and will also cause skin irritation.
Rasta man (p. 163)	A Rastafarian, one of a religious group who believes Emperor Haile Selassie was God's human manifestation on earth, that the "new world" is a Babylonian captivity for Black people. They have a strong commitment to love and peace.
Mr. Tambo (p. 155)	One of the characters in a minstrel-show dialogue.

IF THERE WERE
NO DAYS,
WHERE WOULD
WE LIVE

I

*What's the use of playing the
game if it ain't fun?*

—MAGIC JOHNSON

After That

Every story has its lean meat
and its solid church
so he started to rape her for years.
However, owls close their eyes
in the daytime
because they're awake all night,
and she waited for him
at the handle of his hunting knife
the bells ringing afterward
with the kind of lust
she's always known.
After that her flights were silent
and her voice, of rats and mice.
I don't understand sorcery or omens
even eyes as penetrating as hers,
but under her feathers
and all along the tips of her flight
where she's let me touch her,
I've kissed her fright.

Yellow Sweet Clover

When I hold you in my hands
you rise up out of the water
like a mule deer.
I wish I had yellow sweet clover
from the rim of the river.

At Colm's Foot

If we sit together
in front of the barn
in the only clothes that we own
and don't move,
we will become a group
the camera will remember
as slaves no longer.
The light on us will have that glow
that freedom has
and we will have that little dog
at Colm's foot
as an emblem of the love that binds us.

The Waterfall

I want to ask her
why she bends over
to brush her hair,
but I find myself
coming out of the closet
into a small clearing
with a waterfall
and the longer I look at her
the longer I get wet.

Anniversary

When she walked by
the first time
something happened to him.

When the babies wouldn't come
out alive
he simply drank her tears.

Now that she's feisty with cancer
she likes to make him laugh.
He likes to comb her hair.

The Sniper

That night
when the sky showed me
every star it had
and the biggest moon
I'd ever seen,
I aimed my gun
for the first time
and shot him.
Being nineteen
I rolled on my back
and chewed grass
and counted everything carefully.
Now when my students ask me
"What are their names again?"
I wonder who will forgive me.

There Are Always Fish Here

I keep remembering the date;
it's like the large rock
in the middle of the stream
he likes to stand on.
Tall trees near the bank
on his left
wildflowers to his right
glamorous in the riparian...
1807
"Witnessed a large-scale
transportation of African slaves today."

I wonder if he can see that far
when he casts.

Signing

This is the story
about the flock of birds
that is always flying in your language.

Sometimes, darling
when the weather is bad
and there are plenty of clouds
it looks like they've lost their way.

But then you smile
and I seem to find them anyway.

Why

On those nights
when one of us
is a leaf
and one of us
a bug,
when everything we say
moans or trembles
until we're soaking wet
in a still pool of midnight,
I realize why
in the myth of love
all our guns
and terrible words are flung
into a simmering forge.

May, Age 2

She opens the door
for the joy of the wood.
The solid mahogany
is a skin to her,
her fingers love –
her thumbs
the little bloodhounds in the group.

Dancing with Wolves

We've become the place
where the children kill children
and our gods
still let the sun shine
and the crops have rain,
and then there is the grim reaper
our fashion plate for the innocent life.
They hunt each other
as lonely as we hunted the buffalo away.

Water Carrier

The water carrier
has your skin
has stolen your wrinkles
your flute voice,
and so the fruit trees
in the valley are fed,
and so she walks toward me
without a sign of war in her hips
a sweet community
well fed.

By the Mule River

In the middle of crossing a meadow
by the Mule River
I am stopped by thoughts of you
as moist as your tongue,
and turn east...
The morning sun is like an index finger
on the top of everything,
the flowers are rowdy gems
and I am suddenly rich...
I think about the flowers of you,
the miles and miles of open fields
in jubilant blooming...
I reach for the flowering of you
that goes on and on
and for the buds they come from...
I reach for the stem
and the roots and the seeds themselves
until I am back at the moist earth...

Thoughts are only open arms, I know,
but that's what I did for a while
this morning.

Ripe

1 small ripe papaya
(*about your size*)
peeled, seeded and cut
into ½ inch cubes
(*alive to the touch*)
1 tablespoon
strained fresh lemon's juice
(*in your hair*)
1 tablespoon fresh hot
chilies seeded & cut in strips
⅛ inch wide & 1 inch long...
I am after your oils
and your juices
the things that make my skin
tingle and my eyes burn.

Aubade

This morning
The sun's rays are the galam,
The wooden stylus,
That staggers away from sleep.
Suddenly
I feel the hairs of your arm
Dance with my face.
Touch is a road
To the heart
Across native land...
May nothing ever smell like you again
But rain.
May nothing ever be as silent as you again
But rain.
You are my soft love
My food and drink
My vibrant drum this morning,
And I am your tramp
Rising early with the dusty road
And the bird life
For your love.

Call It What You Want

It is a miracle
If you are swept away,
And it is a miracle
If when you land on your feet
You land like the snowflakes.
Loving her has set you free...
From where you came from
Your blood now has a compelling song in it
Call it what you want...
The eloquence of her lips
Her weapon tongue
Cooing in the wilderness of your ears
Or the spasmodic dance
Undulating in her dress.
You are now much more
Than you thought you could be
Again my man
Startled from the dark pits
Of yourself
Into a luscious life
And though you have a body
It seems to be gone.

Obsessions Are Important

1   I am just the warm water
In your hands
If you were to bring me up
To your face
It would be a blessing.

2   I watch your feet
Cross the floor as I dangle
Off the bed.
I think of mice
In an old farmhouse.
When they get close
I think I'm a cat.

3   I cannot tell
Where the oil begins
And your back ends.
I can only tell
What soft is
And what it does to my heart.

4   When I discovered no one had ever
Loved your knees before
I wanted to build elaborate staircases
All over the world
But I couldn't do that.
Then I began leaving small
Gleaming things lying
On the floor
And finally I began to discover what
Words made you cross and uncross
Your legs.
Obsessions are important.

5   Whenever I suck your breast
    I know you are looking at me.
    I can feel it in your breathing.
    What are you looking at,
    The pattern of my balding head
    The arroyo down my back
    That leads to my butt?
    And what are you thinking about,
    This large hummingbird at your feeder?

6   Your mouth is such a warm bowl
    I can bathe in it.

7   When I finally staggered
    Out of your hair
    I realized I had been wandering
    Around in the woods for hours.

8   There is a reason I have turned into a
    Comfortable chair,
    There is a reason the brass lamp next to me is
    On
    And the glass table has the right size book,
    A slice of bread and a bowl of chowder,
    There is a reason it is raining today
    And the fire is blazing:
    I would do anything to get you into
    My lap.

9   I like to clean out your ears
    With my tongue like they are
    Little jelly jars.
    After all, what are tongues for?

10 You ask me smiling
    Why am I this way.
    I think it is because
    I am a hungry bear
    And you are simply honey.

11 But in the end
    What your vagina has taught me
    Is not simple or soft or warm
    Or delicate or wet.
    It is that the heart and mind
    Cannot thrive without trembling.

Ironing

I opened my history book one day
In the eighth grade
And it said,
This country loved race,
And it ate it
Like warm bread,
And when it finished eating it
It smiled at me
And drank
That huge glass of milk
It always wanted me to drink,
Because it said
It would give me
Strong bones.
If it wasn't for the strong bones
I already have
In that damn story of yours, son,
My grandmother ironing said,
I wouldn't be here.

Lemon Verbena

The point is
She is actually in the air,
Sweet morning air
Out there somewhere
Holding hands with
Running water so clear
You can't believe it.
Watching her cook
Is better than kissing her;
It places me on a ridge
Above a river.
I step up to the edge.
My toes hang over
Exposed to my own fears.
If I were to dive from here
Right now
It would be
Trying to breathe in
Her entire world.
It smells so good –
The peppered bacon
The jumbo eggs and warm bread
As soft as her precise hands
With the aggressive hint
Of lemon verbena and light musk.
And from some cyclically
Recurring condition
Of sexual excitement
All the way down
I could bugle like an elk
For the smell of her.

Ars Poetica

At the edge of the forest
In the middle of the darkness
There is a hand,
As cold as copper,
Like a river
Stretched over wide stones.
Despite the hard rocks
And the furious wind
I love her
Like a flock of birds
Or a mild herd come to drink
For the exquisite rage
And sleek moss of her art.
There is something about a poem
That is violent
That is just another way to die,
Each time we realize our mysteries
We are weakened.
When I am writing I often scatter
Across a lascivious empire
Of passionate flowers.
They all seem so subversive
Even the ones with all their clothes on
They are so obsessed with the minute
Implication of who they are.
I believe if there is a struggle
It should go on
Where real lovers are.
I no longer regret
That I have smelted into one piece
For the sake of this poem.

¿Qué Pasa?

The distance between all the stars
In you
Is soft and black.
If I don't get back soon
Don't call for me
I'm in there, somewhere
Like a new moon
And my stillness is a hunger
Cunning as a wild animal –
Yes indeed.
And I promise you
That unlike the jackal
I will not rob you
Of your goats and chickens,
And in that long time
When it appears nothing is happening
I have broken into minute fragments
Hoping to see more of you...
What a stupid man I have become tonight.

All This

Sometimes
Where the river turns north
Like a small-print dress
It hurts.
All I can do
Is see you there
As suddenly as an evening storm
Your hair
Partly over your face
Before you're gone.
I think
Love is like lightning
The sky of us attacked
So thoroughly
Our cracks show
And what is so absolutely red about us
That we call it the heart
Tends to rumble so profusely
It must have found the various ways
Into our heavens and hells.
I see all this, now
As clearly as if the water
In front of my hands moving off
Is a last kiss.

The End of the Beginning of the Story

I have
Always admired
The spring
Version
Of what really
Happened…
      the snow melting
      the sap rising one –
Where a great deal
Has simply been added
Over the years
And a great deal
Simply removed
      or lost
After a while,
Where things have been left out –
Because,
And a lot been written
That never happened
Except the aim of it all.

Nelson

I thought it was the Olympics
as I watched the gracefulness
with which he stepped up to the
edge of the platform to dive into
the train.

Well-dressed men
who are older brothers
have been known to do strange
things before...

But Kenny and I were just trying to
get through high school
and play football
not understand him.

One thing I did know for sure though
Nelson could paint
the most beautiful pictures
of people with deserts in their eyes.

Maps

Here on the floor
Making maps
Out of our nakedness
There is a sudden willingness
In her warm hands
To dive at the lamp
Like a moth
As if love is always a sacrifice.

Kindling

It was her lightning
that started their
kindling going
and what they had stored
and dried
for years
began to glow.

Good Night

Good night is the richest darkness
I have ever known:
My grandfather's whiskers
My father's chest
My mother's breast
My grandmother's breath
My cultural past
My real tribe
My starlit myths
My wives' hearts
My children sleeping in my arms
The end of love itself.

Things That Are Like Butterflies

I could start with you—
the way you come to me
the way you go away.

Fire Starters

Night is tonguing its way
into the room
the way you do
and I am building a fire

Lists

Anger, the water boiling
Fear, the door closed
Sorrow, the things you will not see begin
Patience, a turtle that climbs mountains
Joy, otters at the river anytime
Smiles, ancient forms of justice

Teo & Monacita

It is essential that a suave man
has a dark, silk shirt
and a wide-brim hat
and when he dips
his lady dancing in his arms
the world of butterflies
in her dress flies loose.
His trimmed mustache.
Her tied hair.
Love is a tawny, sweet thing
when Teo and Monacita dance.

Getting Ready to Talk about Metaphors
& Similes on Valentine's Day

1. You are like the bowl of fruit
   sitting in the morning light
   on the windowsill

2. You are the full moon
   coming out of the clouds again

3. You think about things
   as slowly as the Mississippi does

4. You are as graceful when wet as a waterfall

5. You are the rare black orchid in the show

6. You are as still as a hawk's eye

7. You can roll in your humor
   like a lioness

8. Your eyes can be as far away as the stars

9. Or as near and large as Pyramid Lake

10. Eagles fly
    horses run
    dolphins swim
    but you're more exciting
    than them all

A Story

Her sorrow was the size
of the widest part of the river
The Things You Do Wrong
That Hurt People
Because You Don't Know
What Else to Do,
but that was the rain season
and things changed.

Listening to the Curandera

I wish I knew every spell of the curandera
exactly what to do with flame and smoke
to make it talk
the correct way to talk to the new corn
how to nail the east wind to the door
with four charms
or balance senita spines
on black stones set in Aztec gold
be birdlike in my feelings
for things on the earth
that are really dancers
smile with my face in a variety of mosses
or bear-grass water
or how to snake my way into hidden thoughts,
but I will not need the rest of these reeds
I will not need the rest of these roots,
these grasses, this meat, these berries...
If I am devout, she said,
there is no end to her.

Wind

Every draft of wind begins in serenity
even though there are mountains
and caves that take deep breaths
of it and birds that fly
in it like choirs of angels
and water that moves with it
like a woman dancing in a silk dress.

The Marathon

At the eighth mile
my daughters start to pull away from me.
I smile.
Soon in the large hand
of this ambitious sun
I will be far behind
in the irony of all this,
seeing as how where we're really heading
I'll get there first
and that's cool.

The Wily Cover-Thief's Tale

Walk in the water
where the water almost wins
Walk in the water
when its touch is more than love
Walk 'til the water whispers
Walk with a squelching music
through muddy water
Walk for a long time
barefoot
'til the land is dry
Walk with a stick
Walk backward
Walk and walk and walk
on your hands and knees
Walk nearby but raise no dust
Walk
when night is absolutely priceless
Walk naked if necessary
invisible
Walk with your heart a grasshopper.
You are in a war for the bed for the night
and it will be said
you were the beloved
only if you survive the difficulties.
Then you will awake, happy
and beautiful again.

II

*It is easy to become a human being,
but it is difficult to act like one.*

— TAGALOG PROVERB

If There Were No Days,
Where Would We Live

SWEETNESS,

Will be on the go
wanted you on the go
with me
but you know
how the wind blows
in mythology
and what it does
for a horse like me
kept at grass
it's in the timothy
and the purple moon grass and the fescue
that I love you
but to roll you in the white clover
in wheat
when I get home
will be pure joy.

When the Norse spring began
Freya rode her horse across the world
scattering flowers
this story echoes into Lady Godiva
who lifted the burden of the tax
by riding naked
but horses also bring
the death they've seen
the dragons
who live under the hills
the spider-women
living in the canyons

and in the war
I felt the girth
and the fit of the reins
of death.

Five o'clock had her paintbrush
out again this morning
I saw the red story
beginning in the highlands
in the Apache plume
in the white geranium
that scented air
that smells like you,
but afternoon
was another story,
more animal than usual
coming out the pass,
more savory.

Tonight, however,
if you look at the heavens
with its constellations
with its promise
with its witness
you could see my palm
like a full moon
left-handed in its intuition.
If you breathed on my fingers
they would flex
for the delight of the story.

SWEETNESS,

The thumb is always Uranus
individual from the get-go
persevering but open-minded
and like a child's trick
the index finger
just doesn't like to take orders,
but is an extraordinary leader.
As for the middle finger
the one lovers can't do without
Saturn doesn't mind being alone
doesn't mind the woman in us all
next to the ring finger
the capacity for joy
for happiness with work.
The Venus
no anger
no conflict
in the living by the little finger
that dashing gambler
that bagman
that Zorro
the Mercury
between the mortals and the gods.

SWEETNESS,

Look at the moon tonight
think strawberry papaya
and take this spell with you
your own personal brown-eyed
Buddha
to dream with all night.

In the land of the poem
it's morning
and the first thing I can hear
is the warm water coming
across the floor like you.
Today
I will be headed into the Old Women Mountains
those elegant beige dresses
with the sheer green spots
and as a present from you
I will take orchids
and these cirrus clouds
but first I'll bathe
in the river
sinuous as you
your hero in the buff
starting his journey
with only the scent of you
in the land and the water.
I don't think I'll walk anymore
or lope
for miles today my rhythm
will be pure horse
easy in the nostrils
easy in the running gait
clopping until I get
to the place of loose rocks
before dark.

(*sometime in the afternoon*)

SWEETNESS,

It is so easy to sneak up
on a man
and bring him endless quiet
and beatific joy,
but if they are angels
and I know I have killed angels
for some of the faces were young
their hands smooth
and their hearts soft
and their blood deep lake water.
Dying is a dance of love
if you grab them right
but on a day like today
the river westward & starved
for rain
I am just left with expertise
with where to put
the blade in the throat
the exquisite shot.

Lately the shots have been coming up again
slowly like you start a fire
then the seething, wild flickering
and the robust burn.
War is so exuberant.
I am stunned by what I've done
and how well I did it
and how I grew to love it
want it enormously
like I want you.

I am that man too.

After the war they said Dad loved to bathe.

Nailed him is more than talk;
it is an exquisite gift of pain.
It is said and followed with a laugh
from the deepest part of the throat.
But they didn't
and when he got back with the others
the only one left from the squad
was Morales
his head forever a shot missing the target.

(later)

The path has finally leveled off
at Hooter's Crag
now to the viaduct
then the mill.
Stone grinding against stone
makes me think God isn't listening...

I don't know why I said that.
Perhaps it's that story you told me
about the friend who woke up
finding the darkest part of the night
her father in her,
his eyes the pulsating of the stars,
war is that kind of end to trust.

You said she never wanted to be pretty
again,
matted her hair
tore her clothes
used every odor she could find to hide in
until her father died,
then she became beautiful again…
Today
that story saved my life.

Like the ole folks say,
"That's the way I got over."

There is nothing more beautiful
than coming out of a canyon
water around you,
the temperature slapping your face
like it was a baby's ass,
otters & porcupines hovering
like the opposite ends of grace.

One day I spent ten minutes
sighting a girl planting rice.
It was like she was weaving cloth.
I touched her deeply
and I didn't know her name,
but it is the kind of bouquet
you keep.

Tonight is a fine old lantern.
If love can be made
it's being made.
In the song they say,

"I'll be grass around your finger."
Sweetness...
I'll be grass around your finger
or any afterglow that lasts all night.

FELIS CONCOLOR,

My cougar, uniform color,
one by one the snowflakes came like suitors
wooing the ground
but I was not cold
because I was not chosen.
I was deep in my bag
thinking about the fish you are,
the bear dreaming you again into the water
then looking at you as if you were there.

Magic on the ground, magic in the air
wash my hands like a prairie dog.
Roses and lilacs spend the night blooming,
we will have children,
but today is the hill country
and the sun with its feather duster
until the waterfall.

(later)

FATHER,

I am at the waterfall
of the first woman I have ever loved.

        Thank you.

LUSCIOUSNESS,

Beautiful in motion, beautiful at rest.
Let me be the dew on your face this morning,
and all the time it takes
to get you up slowly
to suggest you move
open up
address the light
all this moisture just for you.
Good morning.
If I am acting like a god
it is because for a year and a day
I could take as much life away
as I could.
Patriotism it is called
syllables that allow you
to endure the unendurable,
but it is going through that channel
into someone else's life
which is God too.

I love you
from the life line in your hand
to the girdle of Venus,
close it around me into a fist,
when the talons come out
we will be falcons together
suggestions gliding together as freely as jazz.
It is not how long we live
but how enthusiastically
we dive
into what we want,
willingness is such a big kiss.

Let me tell you a story...
Hunting is a prayer I know
and I've been hunted
followed by the snapping twigs I broke
when I broke them and why.
The lay of the wild grass
and the best place to find water.
The patrol was wiped out
Ike was on point
& Rivers was into jokes.

We shouldn't have been laughing
but then we were really scared little children.
I'm not sure who tripped the wire
but the show started
beautiful lights, color extraordinary.
Then we started to die —
a leg here
a throat dangling out of a mouth
blood like mud or dough
and they wonder why men dying holler "Mama."
Tyree was stunned without his feet.

I was the only blessed one
blown out of the garden,
slipping from temple to temple.
Never ask why do people die before you
or on top of you
or beside you,
just haul ass.
For a long time nothing moved.
Some men moan longer than they live.

When Byron realized we were the last
and he was next,
he winked.
"City boy, it's ring-a-levio time,
party hard and so long."
He died with the bravado of a ring-necked pheasant
and I was gone on the A train.
In the end the jungle was just another playground
& we boys were playing
for the chance of a hero's life –
cut in here, dodge, lie still
when they are within touching distance
and sometimes
just closing your eyes
and saying the rosary until they're gone.
I was running inside the legend
of every deer I ever killed
churched in the memorial service
for birds hit on the wing.
Fear is the kind of service we can all come to –
grace rolling the dice at the doors.
No sweat stinks like fear.

The childish fantasy of cut & dodge
suddenly was a crucial law
honoring the memory
of every alley
I've ever ran through.
Now I saw leaf,
tree, grass, and stone
like the real animals we are
the stalkers and the stalked.
Then, good luck, Bubba,
you're not in a vegetarian world.

In an hour,
in the middle of silence
with an empty gun,
I took out a stick of gum
for seasoning
and made believe it was you...
After that I preferred to walk point
wore my rosary
and became humorless.

(later)

Passion and anguish,
fear and rage,
have kept me strong enough
for this desert.
In fact I'm blooming like the ironweed,
the cat's claw and the mesquite.
I am at last the crucifixion plant,
the canon dudley and the wily
Joshua tree
home
to see you first as an apparition
in moonlight
then the opening of a hand
that reads in deep, wide lines
the organization of a spirit.
My *Big-Time Fighter*
crossing the bridges of our years apart,
Semper Fidelis.

SWEETNESS,

This morning I am in sight of the Eastern
             Mountains.
The snow left
the pines green gems.
The birdsong is dancing like your voice
across a sky that is as clear
as a crystal ball.   .
Today I will have to cross that rickety bridge
that's like a period of foreign domination
then head for the flats
then the texture of the river bend
and the cattle grazing grasses
that would make a perfect dress.
It is hard to get home with seduction everywhere.

       (later)

I ate at the fire of a strange people
who have money
and say art and education
cost too much
and wonder why we die
of heart trouble
and are annoyed
that our leaders always quarrel
even though they seem to have ears...
I'm glad you have ears,
one for small gifts
and one for something else.

It's getting hot
and there are no Popsicles
or your toes.

SWEETNESS,

Tonight, which one of us is gypsy,
you there
or me here reading your palm?

(morning)

In some countries
when the sun comes up
they can't believe it.
In some countries when it does not
they are lost.
They are like our children
the ones we haven't had.

(later)

Fishing is so romantic
the lure, the line, the catch,
the hanging on for dear life,
and today the river has that face
a baby has after tit,
but all the rivers have been rising
here
and it's been raining
in batches of days.

You get the feeling
these people have done something wrong
that's being set right again
if you've read mythology.
There was a time,
the guy from the barbershop said,
when everyone around here danced
even the old ones moved gracefully
about each other like butterflies.

The heart line begins
on the thumbless side of the palm
traveling horizontally under the fingers,
when it is clear & deeply etched
you have deep emotions...
so the war is over, my love,
and we have killed enough of them,
torched their homes
trampled their fields
mutilated their arms
burned their legs
harvested their ears
and wore them like dark pearls
drove them crazy
made night a sure sign
of death
their schools, lost canyons
with nothing blowing through them
and an exact count of
dead mothers
dead fathers
dead children
and all that was given
taken away.

What do you do now
with the hunger
and the poverty glaring in their faces?
St. Teresa
would have probably kissed it,
but we were not saints
we were soldiers
hiding in the enemy's world.
How many times
must I be dipped into the water
to be a child again?

There was a village
where children loved to play
with kites.
You came to it over a hill
and the first thing you saw
kites —
red and blue birds
multicolored dragons breathing fire
bugs with fat wings
and fat noses.
The kite maker was an old woman;
I loved her wrinkles.
I found out
if you come at the right time
of year
she'd be flying kites
to a dark-haired child
with huge eyes.
They say she has recreated
what she's lost
from the little pieces
she puts back up into the sky.

SWEETNESS,

The shadows are always shifting
their emotions to difficult themes.
Take this morning
when I went down to the river
to bathe
and I heard the women in the oaks
talking about a woman like you:
fresh picked greens,
nuts and fruits and flowers.

I am near that elaborate house
where all the people killed themselves.
They said they were angels
on their way back home.
I can understand how it feels
to want the hand of God to hold onto
when it's excruciatingly painful,
but it is also true
that all the angels are gone
and we are the women and the men
that they've left
with only each other's hands
to hold onto.

The moon is only that illuminating cat,
that gracefulness
along the edges of your sleep
that soft companion
settled comfortably in the dark
moving you
like it moves the tides

to move.
Think of me this way,
and when you wake up
if you go to the place where you first kissed me
and look south
you'll see me coming into the meadow.
I'll bring the meat,
you bring the seasoning.

to be continued...

About the Author

Primus St. John was born in New York City and raised by West Indian grandparents. He has worked as a laborer, gambler, and civil servant, and for the past twenty-six years has taught literature and creative writing at Portland State University in Oregon. One of the five artists who inaugurated the NEA's Poets in the Schools program, St. John has received wide recognition for his poetry, including a reading on National Public Radio, an Oregon Book Award for Poetry, and a nomination for the American Book Award. St. John's titles include *Skins on the Earth* (Copper Canyon), *Love Is Not a Consolation; It Is a Light* (Carnegie Mellon), and *Dreamer* (Carnegie Mellon); he is also co-editor of two notable anthologies, *Zero Makes Me Hungry* (Scott Foresman) and *From Here We Speak* (Oregon State University). He lives in West Linn, Oregon.

The Chinese character for poetry (*shih*) combines "word" and "temple." It also serves as raison d'être for Copper Canyon Press.

Founded in 1972, Copper Canyon publishes extraordinary work — from Nobel laureates to emerging poets — and strives to maintain the highest standards of design, manufacture, marketing, and distribution. Our commitment is nurtured and sustained by the community of readers, writers, booksellers, librarians, teachers, students — everyone who shares the conviction that poetry clarifies and deepens social and spiritual awareness.

Great books depend on great presses. Publication of great poetry is especially dependent on the informed appreciation and generous patronage of readers. By becoming a Friend of Copper Canyon Press you can secure the future — and the legacy — of one of the finest independent publishers in America.

For information and catalogs

COPPER CANYON PRESS
Post Office Box 271
Port Townsend, Washington 98368
360/385-4925
coppercanyon@olympus.net
www.ccpress.org

THIS BOOK IS SET IN ADOBE CASLON, designed by Carol Twombly in 1989 based on specimens of type cut by Englishman William Caslon in the early 1700s. Caslon's designs were the last of the Old Style types that had dominated printing for nearly three hundred years until they were swept aside in the excitement over modern faces by Baskerville, Bodoni, Didot, and others. Caslon's types enjoyed sustained popularity in America, however, where they continued to be used by Colonial printers for such documents as *The Declaration of Independence*. While there have been many versions of Caslon, Twombly's design was the first for digital composition and includes the entire vocabulary: swash characters, ligatures, alternative characters, and border elements that make it delightful to set and to read. Book and section titles are set in ITC Founder's Caslon™ Thirty.

Book design by Valerie Brewster, Scribe Typography. Printed on Glatfelter Author's Text (acid-free, 85% recycled, 10% post-consumer stock) at McNaughton & Gunn.